Twenty-Eight

SNOW ANGELS

Twenty-Eight
SNOW ANGELS

A WIDOW'S STORY OF LOVE, LOSS AND RENEWAL

DIANE DETTMANN

"A keenly observed story of the sudden death of a husband. The reader feels the grief and the hope that follows."
—Adair Lara, author of *Hold Me Close, Let Me Go*

Outskirts Press, Inc.
Denver, Colorado

In this book, I have used first names of individuals who granted me their permission. Some of the names of people, places and medical facilities in this book have been changed or omitted to protect their privacy. The story is based on how I remember the events.

I walked beside the ocean.

His spirit caressed me.

I splashed tears into the winds of the sea.

I miss him so much.

Will the pain ever go away?

MY NOTE ON THE BACK OF A RECEIPT
JACKSONVILLE, FLORIDA, MARCH 2001

*Dedicated to everyone who has grieved
the loss of a loved one.*

*In loving memory of my husband,
John Hohl
June 28, 1946–June 30, 2000*

Acknowledgements

I would like to gratefully acknowledge Adair Lara for her encouragement and inspiration.

Also, a special thank you to Peggy Lang for reading drafts of my manuscript, to Susan Parker for her support and the faculty at the La Jolla Writer's Conference for their meaningful feedback and encouragement.

Many thanks to the following people who read various drafts of the manuscript:

Dr. Margaret Phinney, Patrick Murphy, Linda Parker, Jane Dunlap, Joella Wilson and Mary Jacks.

With deep appreciation I thank my editor Tara L. Masih for her flexibility, understanding and thorough edit of the final draft of the manuscript.

I want to extend a special thank you to my loving family and many of my friends for their support, which helped keep me moving forward, even on my darkest days.

And a huge thank you to my second husband, Allan, for encouraging me to share my story and whose endless love and support helped me to spread my writing wings and fly.

Contents

Prelude

John and I met in 1971 at the Rusty Nail, a smoke-filled bar in Brooklyn Center on the outskirts of Minneapolis. The Nail was a popular hang out for the bar hopping crowd. Bar hopping, back in the seventies, was like date surfing on the net, but you did it in a car, often your best friend's car. On any given night after working out at the European Health Spa my college friend and I piled into her Chevy Nova. Driving from bar to bar, we looked for the best band, cheapest drinks and the highest number of single guys ready to invite us onto the dance floor. In the noisy bar we sipped vodka gimlets and black Russians, praying the band would pound out a Crosby, Stills, Nash & Young or Creedance Clearwater Revival song, and some hot guy would waltz over to our table and ask us to dance. Fast-paced songs gave us a chance to check out a guy with a minimal amount of small talk or body contact.

On that night of January 15, the band cranked out a high-energy song. From the back corner of the bar John wandered over to our table, leaned down and asked me to dance. His blue eyes flashed as the loud music bounced and rocked us back and forth. When the song ended, we hesitated on the dance floor while the band decided what to play next. A soft chord rolled off the lead guitar player's fingers as the band switched to a waltz. We held out our arms and folded into each other.

A week later, we found ourselves on a local skating rink enjoying our first date layered in long underwear, jeans and parkas. We enjoyed the romantic evening with its bright stars and our breath forming clouds as we circled the rink in conversation. We talked about our childhood growing up in North Minneapolis and our life as University of Minnesota students, living at home.

Skating was followed by coffee at Howard Johnson's restaurant on Central Avenue. We slid into a booth and ordered black coffee. John had recently moved back to Minnesota from California and was unemployed. Out of his pocket, he pulled a small plastic bag of chocolate chip cookies. He grinned at me. "Looking for a job and living at home isn't all bad. It has its rewards. My mother baked the cookies." I reached into the plastic bag. *Great cookies*, I thought, as I bit into the soft chocolate morsels, *And great guy, too.*

When we said "I do" in June 1972, the possibilities of our life together were unimaginable and endless. As the recessional music carried us down the aisle in front of family and friends, our heads held visions of never-ending love. We were committed to our vows and to each other. "Until death do us part" is what we said and we meant it. We imagined our marriage would be like Ozzie and Harriet Nelson's in the 1950s—two children, a two-story home, and nightly evening meals around the dining room table. Our family values, middle-class backgrounds, along with the black-and-white television programs, defined our image of marriage.

I had never lived away from home until I married John. During my four years at the University of Minnesota, my younger sister, Mary, and I shared a tiny bedroom. My little sister often fell asleep to the sound of crickets chirping outside our bedroom window and the *plink-plink-plink* of my Smith Corona manual typewriter as I typed term papers late into the night. Sharing a room with my sister was a temporary arrangement. Sharing an apartment with my husband was a commitment to a long and happy future together. John and I eased into our marriage like a slow dance to James Taylor's "I've Got A Friend."

CHAPTER 1

"Happy New Year 2000"

MY HUSBAND AND I rang in the New Year with friends. After an overpriced dinner at a local restaurant, John's best friend and his wife invited us to their new home for more drinks and dessert. With a fire glowing in the fireplace and a plastic "Happy New Year 2000" banner draped above the mantel, we sat as couples and sipped our drinks as our host wandered through the room snapping photos. When he pointed the camera at us, I leaned into John's soft black sweater. My paper "Happy New Year" crown brushed against John's shiny brown hair as he raised his glass and smiled for the camera. Just minutes before midnight our host passed out noisemakers and clicked on the television so we could watch the silver ball drop in Times Square. We counted down: 5–4–3–2–1. "Happy New Year!" we screamed as our noisemakers clanged and squawked. John and I clinked our champagne flutes and kissed.

After a delicious chocolate cheesecake dessert and coffee, we said goodbye and bundled up for the frigid winter drive home. The car door creaked as John opened it and I slid into the passenger's seat. Shivering, I pulled the seatbelt across my bulky winter coat and clicked my belt in place. John's breath hung as vapor in the crisp Minnesota air as he crawled into the driver's seat.

The engine hesitated, but eventually turned over. The tires crackled as the car pulled onto the snow-covered street. During the long, icy drive home we shared memories of the New Year's celebrations we had spent with our friends over the past thirty years. In spite of the bitter cold we knew 2000 was going to be a great year.

The New Year brought resolutions, hopes for 2000 and, unfortunately, the flu season. For several days John slept in a chair to minimize his coughing as his temperature climbed to 104 degrees. I called the clinic. I told the nurse about John's chronic lung condition that he'd had since birth and that I was worried about him. With the waiting rooms filled with sick patients, the nurse recommended I keep John home and give him Tylenol to bring down the fever.

After I hung up the phone, I stared at John, sleeping in his blue leather chair. I questioned the nurse's suggestion, but within a week, his symptoms faded, and John returned to work. Life was back to normal until one afternoon in April when I walked through the back door. The message machine light flashed red. I pushed the play button.

"This is Lakeside Clinic. Please call us . . ." I froze. My hands shook as I pressed the numbers on the keypad.

"Lakeside Clinic. How may I help you?"

"My name is Diane Hohl I'm returning your call."

"Diane, we admitted John to the ICU around two this afternoon. He drove himself here from work. His oxygen level was extremely low." The nurse's calm voice did nothing to quiet the panic that choked me. "You can call him. He's in isolation so visiting is limited to immediate family only."

I dialed the number I had scribbled on a scrap of paper. After several rings, John's frail voice answered, "Hello?"

"Sweetheart, are you all right?"

"I'm okay. They're just checking me out. I'll just be here for a few days. Could you bring a few things?" I jotted the items on the scrap of paper, trying to keep my hand steady and to calm the tremble in my voice.

"Bring that silver mechanical pencil I use for crosswords, too. I think it's by my leather chair on the end table. I love you, Diane."

"I love you, too." I frantically gathered all the items and called my sister Mary. Her husband, Al, answered, "Hi, Di, how are you?" My scrambled mind ignored the question.

"John is in the ICU at Lakeside Hospital. I'm driving up there right now."

"Di, don't go alone. We'll meet you there." I thought I could face this alone, but gave in to Al's offer. When I walked into the intensive care unit, I knew John was in serious trouble. The nurse at the desk looked up from her computer monitor. "Can I help you?"

"I'm John Hohl's wife." She pointed to a closed door with a sign that read "ISOLATION: Gowns Required."

"Put on a gown and mask, they are on the cart by the door. He's very weak, so keep your visit short."

When I walked into the room, John's face lit up. The sparkle in his blue eyes overshadowed the tubes and monitors surrounding him. My fiber mask and gown blocked the kiss I wanted to plant on his cheek.

"Sweetheart, what happened?"

"Oh, I decided I needed a vacation from work." He smiled and winked. "It looks worse than it is. I'll be fine." I pulled a chair up to his bed. He looked so weak I could barely hold back the tears. When he dosed off to the rhythm of the monitors, I quietly closed the door behind me and peeled off my gown. The minute I stepped into the lobby, Mary and Al wrapped their arms around me. Endless sobs racked my body.

"He's in isolation. It looks serious. What am I going to do?"

Mary rubbed my back. "We're here for you, Di. You don't have to go through this alone. John needs you. Go home, call a substitute for tomorrow and get some rest. Do you want us to follow you home?"

I shook my head. We hugged and I headed for the dark parking lot. My whole life ran through my mind as I walked to my car alone. The breeze that warmed my cheeks carried the essence of every vacation we enjoyed in Carmel, California. The pavement under my feet reminded me of our evening walks to art galleries, restaurants and strolling hand in hand back to the cottage after late-night drinks.

In a daze, I wound the Ford Probe through the dark curves on

Stagecoach Trail. Instead of watching for deer leaping out of the road-side brush, my mind focused on John. In the glow of the high beams on the dark pavement, I saw my husband in his faded hospital gown confined in bed and surrounded by beeping monitors. One by one the drops of antibiotics dripped into the needle taped to his thin hand while the respiratory therapist pounded on his back. As hard as I tried to focus on the road ahead, images of my husband's frail body and plastic tubes filled the space beyond the windshield.

When my car headlights flashed on our garage door, I released my grip on the steering wheel. I slammed the car door shut and listened as the garage door rumbled closed. The back door clicked shut behind me. In the darkness the house felt like a tomb. A few minutes later, the phone rang and my sister's number appeared on the caller ID. "Glad you made it home, call a sub right away and try to get some sleep. We'll call you in the morning. Call if you need anything."

During the days that followed, John's strength improved, the isolation sign disappeared, and all the tubes were removed except for the oxygen line. We filled the long hospital hours with Scrabble and cribbage. *Who Wants to Be a Millionaire* provided a daily diversion from the medications, therapy and vital sign checks. John even found enough energy to figure out our income taxes. I can still see him dressed in his hospital gown, propped up in bed with all the receipts and forms spread out on his tray. Thanks to John's perseverance and the hospital's copy machine we met the April 15 deadline. A few days later the oxygen tube was removed and John was discharged.

After the stress of daily hospital visits, I was relieved to return to my class of fifth graders. A week of having a substitute in the room had left my desk piled high with assignments waiting to be graded, notes from parents and stacks of mail to sort. When the bell rang, my wonderful students filed in with smiles and welcome back greetings. One of the last students through the door was Tanya, my most energetic and social student. She stopped in front of my desk to tell me about the substitute and the students who had caused problems. Tanya always had a smile on her face, but that morning it was wider than ever. She was happy to have me back. Our daily routine fell into place like a precisely set clock. I was glad to have my life back to normal.

CHAPTER 2

Call Someone

RELIEVED TO BE home, John worked hard to get back to his daily routine. He continued to go to work every day in spite of his nights of restless sleep. To celebrate his brother's birthday we invited his mom, his brother and my brother over for dinner. The week before, while we cleaned the house and hauled in groceries, John's stamina seemed to be improving. As we sat around the dining room table with the spring sunshine filtering through the sliding glass door, we shared funny family stories and sipped our wine. After chocolate cake and ice cream, I took photos of John and his brother kneeling beside their mother, flashing their broad smiles at the camera.

Over the weeks that followed, John's energy waned. He struggled to catch his breath after short walks, and in the evenings after dinner he dozed off reading the paper. His cough became more persistent and he lost interest in golf, cooking, his daily crossword puzzles and sharing intimate time with me. One Sunday evening while he was resting, I noticed his fingernails were blue, a sign of a low oxygen level. I wanted to call 911, but he told me he would be fine. I called the nurse line and told her his fingers were blue. Without hesitating the nurse responded, "Get him to the emergency room."

I stared at my husband's listless body stretched out on our bed and told him I was going to call 911. John resisted, reassured me he would be fine and just needed a little sleep. He patted me on the hand and closed his eyes. I let him rest for a few minutes while I paced around the kitchen, wondering what to do. The nurse's voice echoed in my mind. I knew I had to get him to the hospital. When I returned to the bedroom, John's eyes were focused on the ceiling. He turned and looked at me. I rubbed his arm and asked him if he felt strong enough to get in the car. He nodded.

I guided him into the car and drove the Probe as fast as I could along the dark winding roads to Lakeside Hospital. The fifteen-mile drive seemed endless. My pulse raced as I pulled up to the emergency room entrance. A nurse greeted us with a wheelchair and rolled John into a cubicle. She gave John a nebulizer breathing treatment and checked his vitals. At 11:30 p.m. the on-call doctor decided to keep John overnight so they could monitor him and run more tests. Relieved that he would be in the doctor's hands, I kissed my husband goodbye and drove home.

When I walked into John's hospital room the next morning, with the newspaper tucked under my arm, I found him surrounded by nurses and doctors frantically adjusting tubes and checking monitors. In between the nurses' shoulders I could see John thrashing and shaking. I wanted to break through the barrier of white uniforms and hold my husband's hand. Instead, I lowered myself onto the wooden chair behind me. Helpless and confused, I watched as John's agitated body slowly calmed.

The attending doctor explained that John had gone into respiratory shock due to a blockage in his lung. They cleared his airway and put him on a ventilator for breathing support. The doctor made arrangements to transport my husband to a hospital in downtown Saint Paul. The doctor assured me that the hospital was known for its innovative staff, supportive patient care, specialized treatment and state-of-the-art technology. His comments did little to calm me. Terror ripped through me as I watched the transport medics connect John to all the life support tubes and portable monitors.

The hospital chaplain escorted me into a small room and asked if I had anyone I could call. I didn't understand why I had to call someone, but the chaplain insisted, so I called John's brother. The chaplain offered to drive me to the hospital in Saint Paul, twenty-five miles away. I declined his offer and assured him I would be fine. As the Life Link van pulled away from the emergency room exit, I eased in behind it. At the first stoplight they turned on their siren and bolted away. Numb, I sat at the stoplight and watched the amber lights flash until the siren faded in the distance. For some reason, the possibility of John's death did not click in my mind. In an emotional fog, I drove along the busy streets of downtown Saint Paul, slamming on my breaks at red lights and somehow ended up in the emergency room parking lot. Adrenaline pumped through my veins as I wound along the hospital hallways and fumbled my way to the intensive care unit desk, where I found John on a cart surrounded by the Life Link team.

I dashed to the cart and pleaded, "That's my husband, save him. He's all I have." The doctor took me aside and attempted to calm me down. "I know it looks bad right now. Your husband will pull out of this, but his life will be extremely compromised." On his clipboard he drew a picture of steps.

"You see his lung condition is like walking down steps. We can stabilize him for now, but there is no cure." He explained how John's chronic lung disease damaged the air sacs that balance the oxygen and carbon dioxide levels in his blood. When the gas levels in the blood are out of balance it can affect a patient's memory, mental functions and even cause coma. As the disease progresses, a patient often has difficulty catching his breath, which can cause severe anxiety and panic. He asked me if John was a smoker. I shook my head. The doctor jotted a note on the form in front of him. He explained that John's condition made him more susceptible to respiratory infections and that patients often use inhalers, oxygen support, medications and respiratory therapy to help manage their progressive symptoms. He assured me they would do everything they could for John and asked if I had any more questions. I shook my head.

Standing by the nurses' station, I watched as the doctor's back disappeared into one of the cubicles. His words rolled through my head and triggered conversations from the past. During one of our first dates John told me he was born two months premature. Doctors had not expected him to live, but thanks to a young intern's special attention, John survived. In spite of his chronic condition, John enjoyed an active, rewarding life. While we were dating he told me that a doctor had recently said he might not live beyond his fifties. At the time, I hadn't given his comment much thought. We were in our twenties, in love, and fifty was a lifetime away.

Exhausted, I watched the ICU nurses wheel my fifty-three year old husband into a gray, windowless room. Highly sedated with an intubation tube taped to his mouth, John slept motionless for days. Beeping monitors and the voices of nurses were my constant companions as I sat by my husband's bedside, praying his eyes would open. A nurse told me one day that I had to take care of myself. She suggested I take a break and go out for lunch. Knowing she was right, I kissed John on the forehead and rode the elevator to the lobby. The spring sunshine splashed across my face as I headed to a pizza place on West Seventh Street, a few blocks away.

The nurse was right. The break away from the hospital was just what I needed. My mind wandered as I sat alone at an outside table in the sun, eating my slice of cheese pizza. The squeal of city busses along the street and the spring leaves that decorated the boulevard trees reminded me of Manhattan, San Francisco and all the places where John and I had traveled. School children on a field trip filled the sidewalk with their chatter and banter. I thought of my students at school and wondered how they were doing. With renewed hope, I hiked back to the hospital in the afternoon sunshine. The minute I walked into the ICU the nurse stopped me. She told me that while I was gone, John had pulled out the intubation tube. They reinserted it and, to prevent him from doing it again, they secured his wrists to the bed railings.

Seeing my husband bound to his bed and connected to all the tubes devastated me. When the restraints on John's wrists, the beep of the monitors and smell of medical adhesive tape became more than I could handle, I wandered the hospital halls. I tried resting on the couch in the visitor's lounge, but sleep evaded me. Alone in the hospital cafeteria, surrounded by strangers and the sound of clanking plates, I choked down a soggy turkey sandwich and returned to John's room.

Anxiety plagued me at home and at the hospital. Even though I knew John was safe, waking up in our bed without him by my side threw me into hysterical episodes of crying and screaming. A constant tightness bound my body. I worried that the twinges in my neck and chest were signs of a heart attack and that I would keel over in the hospital cafeteria or in the parking ramp. Exhausted, I felt helpless. John was all I had, all I had known my whole adult life.

CHAPTER **3**

On the Mend

SITTING ALONE IN the intensive care unit, I felt guilty taking time away from my students, but knew I needed to be with John. Getting substitutes to cover the class had created stress in the building. When a substitute didn't show up, my colleagues had to give up their preparation time to cover my classroom. Every day as I watched the clock in the ICU, I worried about what my students were doing in class. When I knew recess was over, I dialed the school phone number and the secretary connected me to my classroom. My fifth graders took turns on the phone. They said how much they missed me, asked how my husband was doing and pleaded for me to come back for their end of the year celebration. Their energetic voices triggered tears that stuck in my throat. With my life in chaos, I told them to be good for the substitute and promised I would return to school as soon as I could. When I hung up, uncontrollable sobs racked my body.

With the nurses' dedicated attention, the sparkle in John's eyes returned. He wanted to talk to me, but the ventilator tube locked his words inside. One night before I left for home, I wrote the alphabet on a piece of paper. John pointed to the letters and spelled "I love you." I kissed him on the cheek. "I love you too, sweetheart." Through the stressful respiratory therapy and painful tests John maintained his positive, optimistic attitude.

After almost two weeks in the intensive care unit, the doctor scheduled John for discharge. At the hospital on that sunny June morning, I offered to help John get dressed. Sitting on a chair, he assured me he could do it himself. I handed him his favorite long-sleeved shirt. He pushed his arm into the sleeve and I guided the shirt around his back. The ridges on his ribs pushed against his skin. His hands shook as he buttoned his shirt and then slid his legs into his tan slacks. When he stood up to tuck in his shirt, he lost his balance. I tried to catch him but he tumbled over onto the floor. With my heart banging in my chest, I eased him back onto the chair and asked him if he was all right. John nodded.

While waiting for the doctor, I packed John's few belongings into a plastic bag. Thinking about the tumble, I wondered if he was strong enough to go home. I told John I needed to use the restroom. Instead of heading for the bathroom, I ran into the visitor's, lounge and dialed our attorney, a close friend of John's. The minute he answered I started to cry. I told him the doctor planned to discharge John that morning even though I did not think he was ready to go home. Shocked, our friend suggested I talk to the doctor to see if John could stay in the hospital a few more days or if some additional support was available, like a short-term nursing home or home nurse care. I hung up the phone and stopped in the restroom to wipe away the tears.

Outside of John's room, a nurse stood studying the papers on the clipboard in her hand. I told her how scared I was to take John home. I asked if there was any possibility of getting him into a nursing home for a few weeks until he got his strength back. She told me she would check with the social worker and let me know. The sound of John's cough greeted me as I pushed open the door. Still on the chair where I left him, John smiled at me. I sat on the end of the bed. Twirling a tissue in my hand, I asked him what he thought of the possibility of going into a nursing home in Stillwater for a few weeks before he came home. He thought for a while, looked up at me and said, "I want to go home with you, Diane. Just take me home."

"Okay, sweetheart, if that's what you want, that's what we'll do."

When the doctor finally arrived I told him we lived in a small rural community. Our little town of Afton only had a volunteer fire department and the nearest hospital was ten miles away across the St. Croix River in Hudson, Wisconsin. I asked the doctor what I should do if John had difficulty breathing. Call 911, was his casual response. Anger and panic consumed me as the doctor reviewed the discharge papers with us, scribbled his signature on the bottom and a nurse rolled a wheelchair into the room.

The young nurse explained, "John's lung condition can be managed with a portable oxygen supply, medications and respiratory therapy. Many people even travel and play golf. As he gets stronger, his mobility will improve. He has lost a lot of weight so make sure he eats. Don't worry about calories or fat. Feed him malts, steaks, whatever he wants. Right now just breathing is burning calories. He can consume as many calories as a marathon runner." When she asked if I had any other questions, I just shook my head.

I remember running to the parking ramp to get the car, my stomach churning during the endless wait at the front entrance of the hospital. On June 2, 2000, the nurse wheeled John out the hospital door into the bright sunshine and eased him into the front seat of the car. As the nurse placed the portable oxygen tank in the back seat she bent down, patted John on the shoulder and said, "A nurse will come out to your house in a few days to see how it's going. Call if you need anything."

When the car door slammed shut, the thought of calling 911 loomed in my mind. I looked at John and stared at his thin hands. My handsome, six foot two husband now only weighed a hundred and thirty-six pounds. Beyond the whistling plastic tubes that connected John to the metal oxygen tank in the back seat, I saw the man I loved. His gold wedding band wrapped loosely around his ring finger reminded me of the vows we had repeated twenty-seven years ago. I knew everything wasn't going to be "fine," but I smiled and said, "Let's go home, sweetheart."

He smiled at me and nodded. My hands trembled as I shifted the Probe into drive, grabbed the wheel and eased into the stream of traffic on Smith Avenue. Exhausted, John dosed on and off during the drive home. I stopped at Kmart to get his prescriptions filled, but the pharmacist was busy and said the prescriptions would take at least an hour. Leaving John alone in the car was not an option. I decided to take him home first then drive the ten miles back to town while he rested.

My shoulders relaxed as our brick rambler, surrounded by red roses and mature pines, appeared at the end of the quiet cul-de-sac. The green wrought iron rocking chairs stood empty on the patio. When I turned into the driveway, the scenic Saint Croix Valley's blue sky and lush green treetops welcomed us home. I pressed the garage opener and waited until the heavy tan garage door rumbled to a stop. I guided the car into the garage, next to John's black Eagle Vision and eased my husband out of the passenger's seat. I lifted his metal tank out of the car and held the kitchen door open as he walked behind me, pulling his tank behind him. Shortly after John stretched out to rest, I heard a *beep-beep-beep*. A huge delivery van backed into the driveway. The man rolled up the back door of the truck, pulled a ramp onto the front step and wheeled a large metal tank into the front entryway.

"Good afternoon, m'ame. Where do you want the oxygen tank?" Thinking the tank was a temporary part of our life, I directed the delivery guy into the den down the hall from where John was sleeping. The man wheeled the huge tank into the den and attached a plastic tube long enough to reach into our bedroom at the end of the hallway. The deliveryman quickly explained the gauges on the top of the tank, the oxygen level indicators, how to fill the portable tank and the delivery schedule. Before he walked out into the bright July sunshine, he handed me a sign with bright red letters: "No Smoking Oxygen In Use." At that moment I realized our life had changed forever. There would be no more romantic evening walks on the beach in Carmel, no more hikes on mountain trails in Aspen, Colorado, nor the sound of our canoe paddles dripping water from the pristine lakes in the Minnesota Boundary Waters.

John never returned to work. Oxygen tank deliveries, nebulizer treatments and doctor appointments filled our last days together. Other than a nurse who came in to check vitals a couple of times a week and a physical therapist, we were on our own. Every morning after medications and breakfast, I helped him get dressed in cotton slacks and a long-sleeved shirt. His portable tank with its annoying moan followed him like a shadow everywhere he went and was a constant reminder of a potential 911 call. I wrote the neighbor's phone number on several sticky notes and placed them by all the phones in case something happened. One afternoon, after mowing the lawn, I went to check on John. He was not at the dining room table penciling words into his crossword puzzle. I checked his blue leather chair in the living room; not there, either. Panic engulfed me. When I walked into the front foyer, I caught a glimpse of him dressed in his crisp green shirt with his oxygen tank by his side.

He smiled as he pushed his back up and down the front door. "I am doing my exercises just like the therapist told me. Twice a day, so I started right away. I don't want to be strapped into a wheelchair plant-ing flower seeds in a paper cup at eighty. This is the only flat surface I could find." Wanting to keep his life as normal as possible he even pitched in on yard work. As I clipped the shrubs and branches from the trees in the front yard, John—with his oxygen at his side—sat on a green plastic chair and threw the clippings into the wheelbarrow. Within a week, his struggle to maintain a daily routine became more and more of a challenge, but John never gave up.

For a change of scenery one morning, we packed ourselves into the car and headed to the local grocery store. The motorized carts were just inside the front door.

"Do you want to try one of these?" I asked.

John hesitated and smiled. "I suppose. I can pretend it's a golf cart."

With the green metal oxygen tank in the front seat, I watched my fifty-three-year-old husband ease himself into the cart. He navigated up and down the aisles as I quickly checked my list and gathered items into the basket on the front of the red cart. On our way to the checkout lane a mother and her blond-haired toddler passed us. John and the little girl met eye to eye, he winked at her, and she smiled back. The spark that connected John and the curly haired toddler sad-dened me. It was like he was saying goodbye and wishing her a joyful life. Standing in the handicapped grocery checkout lane, I realized the motorized shopping cart would be a permanent part of our life. The red flags signaling the end were everywhere. I was only fifty-two and I refused to acknowledge them as much as John refused to fly the white flag of surrender.

A fine line separates hope and denial. We clung to hope. We adapted our lives to the constant whir of the oxygen, daily weight checks and John's extended periods of rest. Piece by piece, small pleasures in our lives slipped away. Our golf clubs stood idle in the garage, our conversations over candlelight dinners disappeared and even his crossword puzzles remained unfinished. On June 10 we celebrated our twenty-eighth wedding anniversary. Our gift to each other was time, laughter and a shrimp scampi dinner for two. The open flame of our gas stove, his lack of energy and the constant flow of oxygen forced John to relinquish his love of cooking. The kitchen was foreign territory for me. Known as the woman who dusted her stove, I stood over the copper pan, sautéing shrimp in garlic and butter, while John sipped his scotch on ice and guided me every step of the way. Over dinner and a glass of chardonnay, we toasted our years together and slurped buttery linguine into our mouths. Life was good.

CHAPTER 4

Another Birthday

TWO WEEKS LATER, we made plans to celebrate John's fifty-fourth birthday. In spite of his extremely low energy level, he was determined to go out for dinner. His declining lung capacity made even everyday activities a challenge. Early that afternoon, I positioned the oxygen tube over the shower wall and guided him into the shower. As he sat lathering his hair, I placed a chair in front of the mirror so he could shave after his shower.

"Can you help me?" I slipped off my robe and gently stepped into the shower. I washed his back, rinsed his hair and handed him a towel.

"Are you sure you're up to going out for dinner? We don't have to go. I can fix something here."

"I'm fine. I really want to go." Getting ready for his birthday dinner drained his energy, but the warm smile on his face was all worth it. That night at the restaurant in Stillwater, he looked so handsome in his blue silk shirt. I hardly noticed the plastic tubes and the whir of the life-sustaining oxygen. Service was extremely slow and John's energy faded. We ate what we could, paid the bill and wound our way out of the crowded restaurant. I lifted the oxygen tank into the back seat and John eased himself into the car. With a crimson sunset on the horizon, we headed for home.

In the morning, John slept longer than usual. I helped him get dressed in his khaki pants and blue long-sleeved cotton shirt. All day he faded in and out of sleep. He dozed in the chair as I heated up a frozen turkey roll for dinner.

"John, are you okay?"

His drowsy eyes struggled to focus on me. "I'm fine, just tired."

After dinner John sat at the table and sipped a glass of wine. "Diane, thank you so much for dinner and everything you do for me. I really appreciate it."

I held his hand and smiled. "Sweetheart, it was only a heat and serve turkey roll. Not exactly a gourmet meal." I squeezed his hand and stared into his blue eyes. His cough broke the silence.

"I know how hard this is for you, Diane. I didn't want it this way."

"John, we'll get through this. We're a team. I love you so much."

"I love you, too."

That night, before I crawled into bed, I adjusted the oxygen tube and fluffed up his pillow. I kissed him on the cheek and pulled the blanket up around his chin. I stretched out next to him, but sleep evaded me. "Are you okay?" He assured me with a nod.

"I'm restless. I think I'll sit up for a while so I don't disturb you." He nodded again. I slipped out of bed and gently rubbed his arm. I edged my way down the hallway to the extra bedroom. The moon's brilliant light wrapped its arms around me. I curled up in a ball and whispered, "God, I don't know what to do. Help me. We can't go on like this. Please give me an answer." The pillow muffled my sobs and sleep finally took over.

Around 3:00 a.m. a panic rousted me out of a deep sleep. Half awake, I staggered down the hallway to the dark doorway of our bedroom. A cold silence engulfed me. I clicked on the light. "Oh my God!" Shocked to see the covers thrown open and John's stiff body sprawled across our bed, I grabbed his arm. His skin was cold and blue. I screamed and ran to the kitchen. Grabbing the portable phone I dialed 911. My hands shook as I unlocked the front door and ran back to the bedroom. The voice at the end of the phone told me to get him on the floor and start CPR. I grabbed his legs and pulled.

"He's too heavy! Can't I leave him on the bed?"

"No. Get him on the floor." I clutched John's cold ankles. I pulled him to the edge of the bed, grabbed him by the shoulders and eased him onto the floor. In my mind I knew he was gone; in my heart I thought I could save him.

"Does he have a pulse?" My hands trembled as I pressed my fingers against his cold neck.

"No! Help me!"

"Start CPR. Check his mouth. Make sure his airway is clear." Trying to follow the voice's directions, I held the phone to my ear: "Tip his head back, blow two times into his mouth, then do fifteen compressions on his chest." My hands shook as I blew my breath into John's mouth and frantically pumped his chest. I screamed at the phone, "Where are the paramedics?"

"They're on the way. Keep going."

I continued the frantic pace. I forced breath into him and pushed on his chest, praying he would wake up. I heard a rib crack, but kept going. I kept pressing and screaming at God to help. The taste of turkey rollups clung to my lips. In desperation, I slapped John on the cheek to bring him back, but nothing helped.

I did not notice the red lights flashing in the driveway. When the emergency team finally arrived, the paramedics took over and the sheriff lead me down the hall to the study. I eased myself onto a chair at John's desk, next to the large oxygen tank. The hallway fixture cast a dim light through the doorway that illuminated the gold badge on the front of the sheriff's tan shirt. His leather holster crackled as he jotted notes on his pad. Numb, I tried to answer his questions. I told him the doctor's name and that John's medications were in our bedroom on the closet shelf. I explained John's lung condition and told him how scared I had been to bring him home from the hospital.

The questions stopped when a young paramedic appeared in the doorway and reached over to turn off the oxygen tank. "We did all we could, but we couldn't revive him. I am so sorry." A heavy cloud engulfed the room and smothered me. The chaplain took me by the hand and guided me into the living room as the sheriff called the neighbor and my family. Trembling, I curled into John's leather chair. I heard my neighbors' voices in the kitchen. They made coffee and tried to comfort me.

The chaplain held my hand and rubbed my shoulder. My voice echoed through the living room, "I should have stayed in bed with him. I could've saved him. I did everything I could, but it wasn't enough. He can't be gone, he's all I have."

"Diane, you did everything you could. Even if you had been in bed next to him, you probably would not have known. Don't beat yourself up. Would you like me to pray with you?" I nodded and folded my hands in my lap. As the somber prayer rolled through my mind all I could see was the image of John's body lifeless in our bed and his blue eyes staring motionless at the bedroom ceiling.

Static from the female paramedic's radio broke the silence that followed the "amen." She stood beside me. Her pants brushed against the arm of John's blue leather chair as she stooped down. "What mortuary do you want us to call?"

I had never thought about a mortuary. I stared out the window and shrugged my shoulders. "I don't know who to call." She suggested a place in Stillwater. I just nodded. She stayed with me until the mortuary team arrived. Before she left she handed me a pamphlet and a paperback book. The words "I Can't Stop Crying . . ." jumped off the cover. I set the book on the floor next to John's chair.

Unlike the flashing red lights on the ambulance, the mortuary vehicle appeared silently in the darkness. The front door opened. Strange voices echoed in the foyer as the sound of leather shoes clicked along the entryway. The paramedic motioned to the hallway. The two men disappeared through the archway. The footsteps fell silent, buried in the nap of our new beige carpet. A black shroud enclosed my husband's body as the gurney thumped across the ceramic tile foyer and disappeared into the darkness. Without a hug or a kiss goodbye, my John was gone.

CHAPTER 5

The Funeral

"CALL YOUR DOCTOR. You need pills." My friend at the other end of the phone was right. With my sister, Mary, her husband, Al, and my brother, Mike, gathered in the kitchen, I clicked off the phone and speed-dialed my doctor's number. His nurse answered and said she was sorry to hear about John. I told her we were planning the funeral and asked her if I could get some medication that would help calm me down. She put me on hold while she checked with the doctor. It seemed like forever, before the line clicked and my doctor's voice echoed in my ear.

"I'll have Bonnie call a prescription in to the County Market pharmacy in Hudson. It's a small dose of lorazepam, just enough to take off the edge." I thanked the doctor and hung up. My brother-in-law offered to drive into Hudson to pick up the prescription. After he left we called the mortuary in Stillwater and scheduled a time to discuss the funeral.

Maybe it was the drugs or denial, because I only remember small fragments of that July morning at the mortuary. I remember sitting at a long shiny table with Mary, Al and Mike surrounding me. The room was cold and dark for a bright summer day. A well-groomed funeral director with a silver name badge, dressed in a dark suit and a perfect tie, sat across the table. A burgundy folder decorated with gray calla lilies rested unopened on the table in front of him.

The young director shared his condolences. He opened the Family Service folder and gave us a list for funeral planning. Puzzled and in a fog I wondered, *Why isn't John sitting at the table with us?* The funeral director talked about flowers, programs and motorcycle escorts. He asked if we wanted a bagpiper. I told him John loved bagpipe music. Yes, a bagpiper would be nice. When he asked if I wanted my husband's wedding band left on or taken off, I hesitated. I told him to let it go with John and started to sob.

My brother-in-law's voice broke through my tears. "Di, are you sure?" I wiped my eyes and shook my head. The director scribbled a note on the planning sheet to remove the gold band before closing the coffin and return the ring to me after the funeral. Then he led us to the casket room. We wandered among the shiny coffins and picked out a mahogany casket with polished brass handles. Al assured me that John would approve of my choice. I signed the four-page funeral agreement. When I came to the "Discount For Prompt Payment" section I checked the "yes" box. The payment date "7/7/00" leaped off the page. My birthday. A one hundred and fifty dollar discount on my husband's funeral was not the gift I wanted for my fifty-third birthday.

I slipped the agreement copies and the pre-interment warranty into the burgundy folder, shook the director's hand and followed my family out the door. When we walked out into the bright sunshine that filled the parking lot, my legs wobbled. My heart raced. Exhausted, I slid into the hot stuffy car, praying this was all a dream. When I walked into the kitchen, I ignored the flashing red light on the message machine and headed for the living room. I stared at John's blue leather chair. It was empty.

Only fragments of the funeral remain as wisps of memories. Waves of humidity suffocated me as I crawled out of bed on the morning of July 3. My sister stood in the kitchen, sipping coffee. "Did you sleep okay?" I shook my head. I searched for signs of John. His favorite chair at the dining room table where he drank his morning coffee, read the paper and worked the crossword puzzle was empty. There was no note attached to the refrigerator saying, "Sweetheart, have a wonderful day. I love you." No sound of his cough. No moan of his portable oxygen tank. An unfamiliar silence filled the house.

I sat on the hearth. "Mary, how will I make it without him?" She wrapped her arm around my shoulder. "Di, you're strong, you'll make it. Why don't you eat something and then we can start getting ready."

Ready for what? I thought, as I pulled back the foil top of the strawberry yogurt and dipped my spoon into the plastic container. Then I remembered—the funeral. Between tears, I choked the smooth yogurt down one spoonful at a time. The tangled bed covers beckoned my return, but my sister guided me into the shower. The warm water and aroma of shampoo that usually filled the shower with the essence of everyday life wrapped me in an overwhelming swirl of dizziness.

I was confused. John would *never* leave me. I shuffled into the bedroom. Mary's voice severed the silence, "What are you going to wear? This is the only black dress in here." Wrapped in my robe, I stared at my velveteen Laura Ashley dress, the only expensive black outfit I owned. With the July temperatures in the nineties, the velveteen dress was out of the question. The day I brought John home from the hospital, shopping for a black funeral dress had never crossed my mind. My sister continued to filter through my closet while I dried my hair. "This one will work." Mary spread the purple silk dress on the bed and left the room. Swallowing one of the white pills my doctor had prescribed, I struggled into my clothes one layer at a time.

My hands shook as I latched the diamond necklace John had given me so many years ago for our fifth anniversary. Standing in front of my dresser mirror, a drawn face with bloodshot eyes stared back. The gold necklace with three petite diamonds clung to my neck. The matching bracelet hung loosely against my thin wrist. I ran my fingers over the worn velvet box. Then snapped it shut, and slipped it into the middle dresser drawer. The small bottle of Chanel No. 5 perfume John gave me for Valentine's Day called out to me from the my dresser tray.

When I pulled out the stopper the fragrant aroma triggered memories of chamber orchestra concerts, dinner dates at the Saint Paul Hotel and vacations by the Pacific. I dabbed the perfume behind my ears and on my wrists, pushed the stopper back in and twisted the bottle shut.

When we pulled into the mortuary parking lot, I looked down at the front of my silk dress. "Mary, there's a stain on this dress."

"Di, that's okay, no one will notice. You look fine."

A calm washed over my body as friends and family filed by with hugs, kisses and condolences. By the time the service started the chapel was full. My niece and my friend's daughter each played a piece on the piano. A friend, who was a member of my husband's Lion's Club, spoke eloquently of John's love for life and devotion to others. I don't remember the words the reverend passed over the mahogany casket on that sultry July afternoon at the cemetery. Except the "amen" that signaled the end. Car doors clicked open and engines hummed. From the front seat of the van, I watched the vehicles pull away, one by one. As Al eased the van onto the pavement, the large white monument that marked the "Garden of the Apostles" faded into the distance.

On that steamy summer afternoon, the little white tablets surrounded me with a soothing haze. I was grateful for my friend's advice during those devastating days, but mostly for the tiny white tablets. The drone of the piper pumping "Amazing Grace" on his bagpipes still wrenches my soul. I do not remember the pastor's words or the expensive appetizers the caterers served the guests. A vague memory of visiting with faceless people as I wound my body among the round tables covered with white linen after the service still lingers in my mind.

᠉᠉᠉

With the funeral behind me, the solitude of the valley that once gave me peace, now only brought pain. For several weeks I slept on the couch to avoid our empty bed. One morning, after a restless night of tangled dreams, I woke up distraught and alone. Gray clouds buried the sunshine and scattered raindrop tears across the window. Standing in the dining room, I stared at the gray river in the distance. Straggly birch trees spread their branches aimlessly across the valley.

As I wandered through the lonely house, I wondered if we had made the right decision to sell our beautiful two-story home in the city. In town there were neighbors close by for support, and bike paths and coffee shops within walking distance. The house was our dream home, the place where we planned to raise a family and spend our lives together. We discovered the city lot one Friday night while driving through a well-established neighborhood lined with English Tudor and two-story Colonial homes. We jotted down the phone number on the "For Sale" sign concealed by the overgrown brush, and John called the next morning. The lot was available and within weeks our offer was accepted. We designed our three bedroom, Cape Cod style house together. We snapped photos of the excavation, the stud walls and every stage of the project, including moving day. With two incomes we financed the house with the plan of being mortgage free within fifteen years.

During our house construction, we lived with John's mother, Ethel. Or "Mum" as John called her. After the death of John's dad, Ethel, a strong Christian woman, found strength in her daily Bible readings and had adjusted to living alone. In her late sixties she even managed to find a job working for a rich woman in the elite Kenwood area of Minneapolis. The day we arrived on her doorstep with all our belongings she welcomed us with a smile and a hug. John and I felt like teenagers living at home. When we woke up in the morning, homemade bread was perched in the toaster and our orange juice stood waiting for us at the kitchen table. After a long day at work, we arrived home to the aroma of pot roast wafting through the kitchen. The table set with Royal China dishes and cloth napkins beckoned us to sit down. The old days of coming home after cocktails with a "buzz on" after our Friday date nights were few and far between.

Our only private space was John's childhood bedroom. We slept in his double bed, surrounded by black-and-white family photos, bronzed baby shoes and assorted "made in Japan" knick-knacks perched on shadow box shelves. Other than our clothes, the only item in the bedroom that was ours was the television on the dresser. All the rest of our belongings were stashed in his mother's attic and closets, and more was piled floor to ceiling in the basement. Thinking the arrangement would only be for a few months, we were grateful to have a place to stay. Cranking up the volume on the television in our bedroom compensated for the lack of opportunities for spontaneous sex on our own couch, in our own house. We figured we could do anything short term, but as the months dragged on, nightmares filled my sleep that we would never get our life unpacked and back in order.

In August 1979, eleven months after moving all our belongings into Mum's house, we were ecstatic when the movers arrived at her back door. As they hauled our furniture out of the basement, John and I muscled our boxes of china and glassware out of Ethel's attic. While the movers unloaded our furniture into our new home on St. Clair Avenue in Saint Paul, we unwrapped dishes and piled them into kitchen cabinets. Packing paper flew out of the boxes. Every so often I stood in the middle of a room, and twirled around, inhaling the aroma of fresh paint as the soft carpet tickled my bare feet. That night we walked from room to room together and toasted our new home with a bottle of champagne. During the months and years that followed, we made love in every room, hoping a baby would soon be on the way and our dream would be complete. The baby never came.

After enjoying our beautiful home for ten years, John's position as a Vice President of Finance at a major insurance company ended. One by one the new president eliminated positions and filled them with new people. He dragged John along until the very end. The day John lost his job still haunts me. I can see him leaning up against the kitchen counter, his silk striped tie loosened, the collar of his white shirt unbuttoned, and his hands in his pockets. His words, "I'm done," stung and sunk into the pit of my stomach the instant he uttered them.

Without children in our future and after months of late night conversations over drinks, we decided to sell the house. Get out from under the mortgage and downsize. Over the years I realized dreams were just that, dreams. When the "For Sale" sign appeared in the front yard, an unexpected shock hit me: the thought of selling the home we loved rolled through my body like the tremor of an earthquake.

Our custom designed house sold quickly. We had an estate sale, and moved into a nine hundred and fifty square foot townhouse in Woodbury, a rural community about fifteen miles east of Saint Paul. This time we paid a moving company to store our furniture until we figured out what in the heck we were doing. We faced moving day together, committed to another change in our life. As long as we were together we could face anything.

We filled our tiny townhouse with our basic necessities and all the art we owned. By the time we finished hanging the art pieces, the white walls looked like a gallery with original oils and prints stacked one above the other. We collected art when we traveled. Most of the pieces we purchased from galleries in Carmel, California, a place we fell in love with the first time we visited it on our honeymoon in 1972. The artwork on the town house walls reminded us daily of the essence of Carmel, the power of the Pacific and our love for each other.

On June 18, 1990, when I began my three-year master's program at Hamline University, I never imagined we would be renting a nine-hundred-square foot town house in Woodbury. Attending Hamline had been a dream of mine since high school, but too expensive. I ended up at the University of Minnesota, a more financially feasible option, and lived at home. When I decided to pursue my master's degree, I attended an information session at Hamline. Before the meeting was over I knew it was the program for me. With both of us working, John and I figured we could afford the tuition. When my entrance scores from the Miller Analogy Test arrived in the mail, I tore open the envelope and screamed, "I passed!" We sat on the couch next to each other, toasted my new adventure with a glass of wine and sealed our commitment with a kiss.

The town house was the perfect place to finish writing my thesis and allowed us time to look for a permanent place to live. Over drinks in the evening we talked about downsizing our lives. John took temporary jobs while he continued his search for a full-time position. On weekends, we studied the real estate ads in the Sunday paper and circled listings that caught our interest. Every week our Realtor sent us lists of properties within a forty-mile radius of the town house. Before John left his position as Chief Financial Officer he negotiated keeping the company car as part of his severance package. On weekends John navigated the compact four-speed Cadillac Cimarron along freeways and gravel roads. He shifted from gear to gear as I studied the directions on the listings and read my assignments for class.

After months of house hunting, an ad in the Sunday paper led us to a home in Afton, a rural town with twenty-five hundred residents forty miles east of Minneapolis. With more space than we needed and an acre of yard to mow, the thirty-six hundred square foot brick rambler-walkout was not suited for our mortgage-free, downsizing plan. However, the moment we stepped out on the deck, the view of endless trees and the cobalt blue Saint Croix River captured our souls. The day we signed the closing papers, we drove out to the house with a bottle of champagne. Standing on the deck we clinked our glasses and kissed.

CHAPTER  6

Alone

BUILT IN 1965, OUR house in Afton needed a serious update. Wallpaper and paneling covered every wall surface in the house. One summer morning, while John was at work, I decided to start tearing off the autumn leaf wallpaper that covered the kitchen and dining room. I ripped a small section off the wall behind the canisters. One piece led to another. The smell of wallpaper stripper filled the room as I scraped my way around the kitchen and into the dining room. Suddenly the phone rang; I stepped over the sticky mess below the step stool and grabbed the receiver.

John's voice popped on the line, "Hello, sweetheart. Thought I'd call and see what you're doing."

I stared at the mess on the floor. "I'm standing in the dining room stripping."

"In that case, I'll be right home."

I could feel the spark in his eyes. I laughed. "You nut, I'm stripping wallpaper." John offered to stop at the hardware store to get paint samples and pick up some Chinese take out for dinner. After we finished stripping and painting the walls, we moved all the furniture back in place.

The paint job led to a complete kitchen tear out with weeks of demolition. The morning after the construction crew ripped out the center-island, dishwasher and stove we found ourselves without water. Having lived in the city for most of our lives, it took us awhile to connect the lack of water with a well problem. We called a local well service company. An hour or so later a red truck pulled in the driveway and an elderly fellow eased himself out of the truck. He greeted us with a smile and introduced himself as the owner of the company. He checked the wellhead concealed under a lava rock and informed us that our pump was probably "down." Not knowing what that meant, we followed him to the basement.

After a quick survey of the circuit breaker box he shuffled back upstairs in his soft leather loafers and announced, "Yup, it's the pump. You need a new one. We'll need to pull all the pipe to get to the bottom of the well." John asked him how much that would cost.

"Not cheap to pull three hundred feet of pipe up. I guess around twenty-five hundred." John gulped. With the pump replaced and the kitchen finished, to save money, we focused on home maintenance projects and repairs we could do ourselves. We ripped the indoor-outdoor carpeting off the family room floor in the lower level, painted the cement block walls in the storage room, and installed shelves so we could store our unpacked boxes.

As we cleaned and organized the lower level, brown crickets jumped out from behind furniture and out of cabinets. The house had been vacant for a while. We figured the crickets were a temporary pest we could control with bug spray. They proved us wrong. The morning I found one staring at me from the bristles of my toothbrush, I grabbed the phone and called a local pest control company. I described the disgusting brown crickets with their hump shaped backs to the exterminator. He told me they were harmless camel crickets and assured me everyone in the valley had them. The exterminator arrived a few days later. When he finished spraying every room in the house I wrote out a check for three hundred dollars for three months of treatments, hoping that would take care of the problem.

The crickets seemed to disappear with the cool autumn days. Relieved, we spent our weekends mowing the yard with our Toro rider lawn mower, cleaning out gutters and removing Buckthorn, an invasive shrub with sharp thorns that covered the bluff. As we settled into the house, John continued his job search. I taught at an elementary school in Saint Paul and focused on completing my master's program. In June of 1993 I received my diploma. I had never had a big graduation party, so John and I invited friends and family out to the house to celebrate. Together we planned the menu. John cooked and I ordered the cake with the inscription, "Diane's Dun!" As the years passed the valley's essence never failed to amaze us. Every season brought us a new panoramic view as the red-tailed hawks and turkey vultures glided above the treetops. In spite of the challenges of living in the country, we enjoyed every day we had together.

♪♪♪

After John died, I called our attorney about selling the house. I told him I was worried about paying the mortgage, all the monthly bills and the additional home improvement loan we had taken out for the remodeling project. He advised me not to make any major decisions for at least a year. A close friend of John's, he warned me to be careful, that there were men out there looking for young widows like me with a good job and a beautiful home. I took his advice and committed myself to staying in the house no matter what, but the financial responsibilities continued to overwhelm me.

During all our years together, John had handled the finances, balanced the checkbook and paid the bills. I just left the Visa slips on the desk and magically the balances were paid. As the bills and credit card statements rolled in after the funeral, I knew I had to face the piles on the desk in the computer room. One night I poured myself a stiff brandy and decided to tackle the bills. It took me five tries to walk into the empty room. I pulled out the desk chair where John usually sat and shuffled through the envelopes. I ripped open the mortgage statement. When I flipped through the checkbook John's handwriting jumped off the page. The phone rang and broke the silence in the room. I tried to wipe away my tears before I lifted the receiver. Al's voice came on the other end of the phone. The minute I said hello, my brother-in-law knew something was wrong.

"Hey, Di, are you okay?"

"No. I'm really struggling with all the bills and paperwork that's piling up."

"Di, just leave it for now. I'll come down and help you sort things out tomorrow night. Once you get a system figured out, it'll be easier." I wanted to handle everything myself, not bother others, but I gave in to Al's offer. After I hung up the phone I stared at the open checkbook register in front of me. I picked up a pen. On the transaction line I wrote, "Sorry Sweetheart, I'll try again tomorrow." I slipped the checkbook in the desk drawer, shut off the light and crawled into bed.

In the morning I felt more settled and decided to run some errands. The bank was my first stop. I pulled into a spot in the Wells Fargo parking lot and slammed the car door behind me. My stomach rolled as I stood in line waiting at the customer service counter. The woman greeted me with a smile. I told her my husband had just died, and I needed help with our accounts. She said she was sorry about my husband and guided me into a little cubicle where a woman dressed in a red suit sat behind a desk. Her name plaque read, "Carol Reed." Her kind smile and soft voice put me at ease. She asked what she could do for me. I handed her a registered copy of the death certificate. After studying our accounts on her computer screen, she changed the account information and set up a money market account for John's life insurance check.

After Carol explained the account information she guided me through the automated phone banking system and gave me the name of a financial advisor to help with the investments. Carol handed me her card and told me to call anytime if I had questions. Back in the car I studied my list of errands. They all seemed so pointless. With the needle on my fuel gauge hovering over "E" I decided to stop at the gas station and leave the other errands for later. Standing in the sun, gas fumes whirled around my head as the numbers flipped over on the gas pump. Exhausted, I clicked my seatbelt in place, pointed the Probe toward Afton and headed home. I felt blessed to have met Carol. Just knowing I had her phone number put me at ease and inspired me to keep going.

With some of the errands behind me, I poured myself a glass of port wine and settled into the wrought iron chairs on the patio. The bricks behind me radiated the heat captured from the afternoon sun. Blue jays screamed from the tops of the oak trees on the far side of the yard. As I stared at the apple tree leaves rippling in the wind, I heard the sound of tires crackling along the road. A car pulled into the driveway and three people got out. At first I thought they were Jehovah's Witnesses, but they did not have any packets or Bibles with them. They introduced themselves as members of Shepherd of the Valley, a church John and I had attended a few times. They told me they were very sorry for my loss. All the memories and shock of John's death welled up inside me. I broke down. They took my hand and prayed with me. Before they left they handed me a card with the church phone number and told me to call if I wanted to talk or needed help.

After the car pulled out of the driveway, I set the card on the wrought iron table next to me. I refilled my wine glass and sipped the warm ruby liquid as I rocked back and forth in the wrought iron rocking chair. Every so often my bloodshot eyes were drawn to the tiny card. The huge black letters G-O-D radiated from the center of the card. I read and reread the words surrounded by rainbow colors, "Put **GOD** in the center—and everything will come together." I wondered how that was possible, considering all of the prayers and pleas for help I had already sent to God. I tipped the last drop of port wine into my mouth and headed inside. I pulled a magnet out of the kitchen drawer and secured the bright-colored card in the middle of the white refrigerator door.

When I woke up Saturday morning, I remembered the RSVP I had sent to attend a wedding for the son of our neighbors who lived across the street from us in Saint Paul. *What had I been thinking when*

I marked the "yes" box in front of "I will attend"? I remembered how hard it was to write the number "1" on the line instead of "2." It was too late to cancel. A neighbor that lived next door to us in Saint Paul called and offered me a ride to the wedding. He suggested I meet his sister and him at the Town and Country Club where the reception would be and leave my car there. I hesitated, but thought it would be less stressful than driving myself. So I agreed.

My hands shook as I showered and dressed. I tried to steady the eyeliner pencil as I drew it along my eyelids. I hoped the shaking would disappear once I got to the wedding, but as a safety net I washed down one of my tiny pills before heading out the door. I drove to Saint Paul and met my neighbor at the Town and Country Club. I pulled into an empty parking space and locked the Probe behind me. I greeted my neighbor and his wife, then crawled into the back seat of my neighbor's black Mercedes and settled in next to his sister. I tried to add my comments to their conversation about the wedding, weather and what was new in the neighborhood. Their voices rolled around in my head while John's face flashed through my mind. Trapped in the back seat, I felt numb and alone.

Even with the tranquilizer coursing through my bloodstream, the anxiety escalated. When we entered the sanctuary, the massive arched ceilings and endless rows of pews overwhelmed me. I felt dizzy as the four of us filed down the endless side aisle heading to the front. Together we slid into a long wooden pew. My plan to sit at the back of the church at the end of a row for an emergency escape faded quickly. Locked in the center between my neighbor and a woman I did not know, I panicked. I glanced back and forth from the altar to the program trying to calm myself while the wedding processional music filled the space around me.

The jewels on the bride's dress reflected the light from the arched ceiling and sparked memories of my wedding day. With the wedding party in place, I sat down on the hard pew while the Catholics surrounding me kneeled and prayed. I tried to focus on the large Jesus crucifix beyond the altar, but it reminded me of John when I found him dead in bed, his eyes, looking to the ceiling, cold and still. I thought of how hard I had prayed for God to save him.

The young woman next to me leaned over and asked if I was okay. I blotted my tears with my white lace handkerchief, shook my head and told her my husband had just died. She wrapped her arm around me and whispered that she would put me in her prayers. I hoped her prayers would save me. As we were filing out of the church the young woman asked if I was coming to the reception. I tried to smile as I told her my husband would be disappointed if I struggled through the wedding and skipped the fun part. She smiled and said she would see me at the country club.

The Town and County Club reminded me of the Lodge at Pebble Beach. The dark woodwork, coved ceilings and paneling drew me back to our trips to the Pacific Coast. After drinks and dinner, the lights dimmed and the dancing began. I wanted John there to hold me. I escaped to the restroom and sat in the stall, wishing I had been the first one to die. The band was on break when I returned. I thanked the mother and father of the bride and headed out the front door. Under the star-filled sky, I walked across the parking lot. Relieved that I had left my car at the country club, I pushed the key into the Probe's ignition and headed east on Interstate 94 toward Afton. I pictured John waiting for me at the back door. But when the headlights flashed against the front of the house, all I saw was darkness.

CHAPTER 7

Changes

IN ORDER TO stay in the house, pay the mortgage and maintain my sanity, I knew I could not return to the teaching position I had when John was ill. Flashbacks of stressful staff meetings, the lack of substitutes to cover my class, and the unpaid time I took off to care for John overwhelmed me. During the months after the funeral I worried about my financial situation. In May 1999 we had decided to complete the last phase of our home remodeling plan. To finance the project we took out a short-term loan and planned to have it paid off within a few years. Now on just my teaching salary, I worried about making the payments.

In August 1999, when I left the school I had taught in for twenty-five years and took a fifth-grade position at another school on the opposite side of town, I never imagined I would be alone a year later. The following May when John became ill, I took days and eventually weeks away from my fifth graders to spend time at the hospital. Leaving my students with substitutes consumed me with guilt. My supportive principal assured me my class would be fine and that I needed to be with my husband.

A week after John's funeral, my principal and Cindy, a teacher who started at the school when I did, drove out to my house with a picnic lunch. We ate on the deck and talked about the stressful school year, and the death of loved ones. I told them Eloise, one of my fifth graders, had called me to tell me how sorry she was to hear about my husband. She had offered to give me a puppy to keep me company, but I had turned down her generous offer. When my visitors packed up to leave, my principal hugged me and said, "If there is anything I can do to help, anything, just call."

I thought for a minute and said, "If you hear of any positions in other schools let me know. I loved my fifth graders, they were wonderful and you have been so supportive. But I just can't return to that school."

She nodded. "I understand. I'll check with other principals in the district. Take care of yourself, Diane. I'll call if I hear of anything." I waved as the car eased out of the driveway.

On July 14, while I was staying at my sister's house in Lindstrom an hour away, the phone rang. Thinking it was one of her kids, Mary grabbed the receiver off the wall. After a quick hello she handed it to me. My principal had a job lead for me. A principal in another school that was recently put on academic probation was interviewing for a Literacy Coach. He wanted someone who had a strong background in reading instruction. All I had to do was call him and set up an interview. I wrote his name and number on a scrap of paper. After I hung up, I stared at the phone. My hands shook as I dialed the number and waited for the voice to answer.

When the man's friendly voice answered, I hesitated. Afraid of getting the job or not getting the job, I wanted to hang up. His kind words rolled around in my head: "With your experience and National Board Certification you come highly recommended for this position. We'd like you to come in for an interview as soon as possible. How about Tuesday morning at ten o'clock?" Panic rolled over me. Doubts filled my head. *What was I doing?* I agreed to the interview and thanked him. After hanging up, I almost called him back to cancel the job interview. My sister said it was a great opportunity and offered to go with me.

On July 17, the morning of the interview, my sister dug through my closet and picked out a simple black dress scattered with white flowers and a pair of sandals for me to wear. She helped me fix my hair and encouraged me to eat a bowl of cereal for breakfast. The thought of interviewing for another new job just weeks after John's death filled me with anxiety. Thankful that I still had few of the anti-anxiety pills the doctor prescribed, I gulped one down with a glass of water.

As Mary wove my red Probe through the freeway traffic, she asked questions so I could practice for the interview. Mary told me to relax and reassured me that I would do fine. When we walked into the building my heart slammed against my chest. I wanted to run back to the car, go home and crawl into bed. Instead, Mary guided me down the dark hallway and into the front office. A jovial man greeted us with a smile and a handshake. Then he escorted me into a small corner office where another man shook my hand and offered me a place at a small, round table.

I settled into a chair across from the two men dressed in short-sleeved sport shirts. The office was crowded and stuffy. A fan hummed in the corner. I calmed my shaking hands by cradling them in my lap. During the casual interview the two men focused their questions on my experience and were impressed with my resume. Anxiety rattled in my voice as I searched for the right words to answer their questions about the state standards and my literacy training background. At the end of the interview they complimented me on my qualifications. The principal said he would let me know their decision in a couple of days after they reviewed the other applications.

All the way home I thought about the interview. *Did I answer the questions right? What if I don't get the job?* A calm settled over me as we pulled into the driveway and walked through the back door. After Mary left, the house fell silent again. With only the refrigerator's hum to keep me company, I slipped off the interview dress, hung it in my closet and crawled into bed with the portable phone. Exhausted from the interview, my tears blessed me with rest.

Later that afternoon, the phone startled me out of my deep sleep. The voice at the end said, "Diane?" My heart pounded in my ears as

I sat up. "I know I said I would call in a day or two, but I wanted you to know right away that we would love to have you on board. Do you still want the job?" For a few seconds the words stuck in my throat. Finally, I choked out, "Yes . . . I do want the job."

"Well, it's yours. Would Thursday morning be a good time for you to come in so we can go over some of the details of the position?" I jotted the date and time on the note pad on the nightstand. I thanked God and prayed for the strength to keep going. I was never sure if He was listening, but figured it couldn't hurt. I called my sister with the news. She was excited about the position and offered to help me pack up my classroom.

The next morning I climbed into Mary's van, clicked my seatbelt in place and we headed to my old school. Buildings and malls whizzed by as we chattered about the interview and my new position. When we pulled into the empty parking lot in back of the old brick three-story building, my stomach rolled over. Panic rolled over me. *Could I handle another change in my life?* We walked in through the back door of the empty school. Flashbacks of my wonderful fifth graders and John lying in the intensive care unit filled my mind. I stopped in the middle of the gray hallway. "Mary, I can't do this. I made a mistake. Let's go home."

"Di, it'll be fine. A change is probably just what you need. Come on, let's get your stuff packed up and out of this depressing place." Mary and I wheeled the last load of boxes down the empty hallway and into the elevator. Crammed in the dusty elevator, surrounded by boxes filled with memories of my teaching career, the guilt of letting my students down consumed me. Unsure of where my new literacy position would lead me, I was moving on.

⌇⌇⌇

The day before I met my new team members, I forced myself to face the forty boxes piled in the garage. Over the next several hours I dug through boxes of reading resources, old notebooks from workshops, and notes from parents and students. At the bottom of one box I found a folder of my fifth grader's writing. Tucked inside, I found the cards they made me when John was in the ICU. The phrases, MISS YOU . . . PLEASE COME BACK . . . YOU'RE THE BEST TEACHER, leaped off the folded construction paper. Their giant words surrounded by brightly colored smiley faces, rainbows and beams of sunshine rolled my stomach into a knot. Abandoning them, I felt like a traitor.

The next morning I crammed several boxes of teaching materials into the trunk of the Probe and headed to my new school. My fifth graders' words filtered through my mind as cars whizzed by me on the freeway. The July sun beat down on the windshield as I turned into the parking lot and guided my car into a spot in front of the gray building. Wanting to make a good impression on my new team, I checked the rearview mirror to make sure any signs of my morning tears were gone. Entering the windowless entrance, I tunneled through the gray hallways, not sure where I was headed. A high-speed fan fluttered the papers on the bulletin board behind the counter as I walked into the main office. The secretary greeted me with a cheerful "good morning" and directed me to the same office where the principal had interviewed me. Laughter filtered through the narrow hallway. I walked into the cramped office.

"Good Morning, Diane. Glad you could make it." The principal's cheerful voice and friendly smile put me at ease, at least for the moment. He looked at the two ladies at the table. "These are your team mates, Jane and Linda." I shook their hands and for the next several minutes we talked about our backgrounds and how we would be traveling together for training. *Training? Oh my God, what had I gotten myself into?*

"Welcome to the team, Diane." He handed me a sticky note with a phone number on it. "You'll have to call this number to reserve a room at this hotel in Washington, D.C. Hopefully it's not too late."

"She can bunk in with me if she can't get a room. I don't mind." Jane smiled at her generous offer. My heart thumped against my chest. The principal offered me his phone. With everyone watching, I tried to steady my hands as I pushed the buttons. A reservation agent answered. I told her I needed to book a room for the National Literacy training session in August. After giving her the dates she asked me to hold. Finally the voice returned, "We have a single room available." Relieved, I read off the reservation account number on the sticky note in front of me. Then I jotted down the room confirmation information, thanked the woman and hung up. The principal smiled and handed me another sheet of paper.

"Well, now all you have to do is call this number for your flight to D.C. and you'll be set." He looked at the clock on the wall. "I've got a meeting, so I'll leave you ladies alone so you can get your office set up. Great to have you on board, Diane."

After he left Jane broke the silence hanging in the stuffy room with an offer to show me "our" office. Trudging up the humid hallway, I followed Jane and Linda to a room with two desks and a few worn shelves. The dark room had one long window overlooking the hallway and a smattering of old furniture.

"We'll have to find you a desk and maybe a file cabinet. Until then you can stack your boxes wherever. Don't forget to call that number for your plane reservation. You can use that phone on the wall. Just dial 9 for an outside line."

I thanked them for their help and headed for the car to unload my boxes. It took several trips to haul my boxes into our office and pile them against an empty wall just inside the door. After I eased the last box onto the pile, I finally mustered up enough nerve to call the number on the slip of paper. Bombarded by too many changes, I felt out of control. All the new faces and voices swirled in my head. Sweat poured down my face and disguised the tears that started running down my cheeks. Finally, the agent's warm voice answered, and within minutes I was booked on a flight to Washington, D.C., with my colleagues.

For the next several hours as the humidity climbed, my emotional stamina dropped. Jane managed to acquire an old wooden desk and a few small shelves for me. I went through the motions of settling into my new space. I dusted off shelves, arranged materials and filled the center drawer of my desk with assorted office supplies. In the last box, I found the picture of John and me sitting on the deck at Ne- penthe's restaurant in Big Sur, California, with the blue sky and the Pacific in the background. His smile reached out from the photo, and I felt his arms wrapped around me. I didn't want to fall apart in front of my teammates. By the end of the day I was physically exhausted and emotionally drained. After saying goodbye to my colleagues, I climbed into the Probe, threw my head back and let my emotions flow. *God, what have I done! I want my husband back. I hate this.*

CHAPTER **8**

Invisible Support

MOVING ON WAS one thing. Speeding ahead into the unknown was something totally different. Without any adult children to call for advice, my brother, my sister and her family became my strongest supporters. They offered guidance as we sat at the mortuary planning the funeral, and they wrapped their arms around me at the graveside. They broke my daily loneliness with phone calls, visits and love. Days after the funeral, exhausted from sobbing, I dragged myself out of bed and escaped to a neighbor's house across the street for a few hours. When I returned, a bag of groceries greeted me at the back door, a special delivery from my brother, Mike. The first few weeks of my new job, Mike called every day at 5:30 a.m. to make sure I was awake. The sound of his voice at the end of the phone helped soften the absence of John's, "Good morning, sweetheart." Mike's morning greeting and words of encouragement motivated me to put my feet on the floor, get in the shower and keep going.

Sometimes support appeared out of nowhere. To avoid the empty house on a weekend, I drove to my sister's house and stayed over night. Mary worked as a design consultant at a local art gallery in Lindstrom, a small town fifty miles north of Saint Paul. During a few of my visits, I hung around the gallery while she arranged artwork and waited on customers. The gallery was filled with almond-scented candles. Aroma diffusers filled the air with the essence of redwoods and eucalyptus. Wind chimes tinkled when the warm summer breeze swished through the front door as customers entered the shop. Peaceful minifountains placed around the gallery trickled in the background as soft music filled the air.

One day, while I sat on a soft cushioned chair reading a widow's self-help book, the eucalyptus scent triggered memories of trips with John to Carmel, the smell of kelp at dawn and romantic sunset walks along the Pacific. The images pushed tears down my cheeks. An old woman stopped in front of me and asked what was wrong. I told her my husband had died. She leaned over and hugged me. She kissed me on the forehead and said, "Let God help you through it, don't resist." I thanked the woman, but wanted to tell her God had not been much help so far.

After Mary finished work, we decided to browse through the "Ragtime Clothing" store across the street. When we walked into the consignment shop, a woman young enough to be my daughter greeted us with a friendly hello and invited us to browse around. Mary suggested I look through the dresses and sport coats to see if I could find something for my new job.

I flipped through the racks of used clothes, confused. *Why was I shopping here instead of at some up scale store at a mall with John?* Nothing made sense. My heart raced. Panic rippled through my body. All I wanted to do was run out of the store, but Mary appeared from behind a rack with several hangers in her hand. "Here, Di, try these on. The dressing room is back there in the corner." The young woman followed us and pulled back the dressing room curtain. I hung the hangers on the hook.

"Let me know if you need any help. My name's Paula. I'm the owner." I thanked her and pulled the curtain closed. Standing in the dressing room, I peeled my clothes off and hung them on a hook. I barely recognized the sad, scrawny shape looking back at me in the mirror. After trying on all the dresses, I returned them to the racks. I tried on a sport coat that Mary found. I was not sure if I liked the floral pattern scattered across the dark background, but decided for five dollars I could wear it with slacks to work.

"Looks like you found something," Paula said. I set the sport coat on the counter and dug my wallet out of my purse. "With tax that'll be five dollars and thirty cents. That jacket has lots of colors in it. You can wear it with skirts and slacks."

I handed Paula a ten-dollar bill. Mary said, "This is my sister, Diane. She's starting a new job in a couple of weeks."

Paula's face lit up. "Great, that should be exciting."

I looked down at the floor. "My husband died two weeks ago."

Paula walked out from behind the counter. She wrapped her arms around me. "I'm so sorry. I totally understand the pain you're going through. My fiancé died a year and a half ago in a car accident." We held each other like old friends and sobbed. Before we left, Paula and I exchanged phone numbers. Whenever I stayed at my sister's, we made a point of stopping at Paula's consignment store to shop and visit. Paula and I supported each other with frequent phone calls. I looked forward to our conversations about loss and how grief sucked. Paula understood; she was like the daughter I never had.

On Saturday, the day before my trip to Washington, D.C., my sister helped me pack as I paced around the bedroom insisting I had made a mistake and did not want to go. She convinced me I *had* to, I had no choice. She assured me I would be fine once I got there. I believed her. Sunday afternoon with my suitcase filled with dresses, slacks and several pairs of shoes, I clicked the locks shut on my yellow hard shell suitcase and double-checked my carry on for my trip itinerary.

My brother picked me up in his '69 Road Runner convertible and drove me to the Hubert H. Humphrey terminal where my colleagues had told me to meet them. As the Road Runner sped down Interstate 494 in the early afternoon sunshine, I couldn't remember what my colleagues looked like. *Were they tall? Short? What did they say they'd be wearing?* Even their names, Jane and Linda, evaded me at that moment. I wanted to tell Mike to stop, turn around and take me home. It was too late! I stood on the curb at the airport. My stomach tumbled like an overloaded clothes dryer. My pulse smashed against my veins. Panic set in as Mike slammed the trunk shut and hugged me.

I watched the Road Runner's taillights disappear into the distance, then dragged my Samsonite suitcase through the automatic doors and into the air-conditioned terminal. Struggling to navigate my way through the crowd, every man's face reminded me of John. My suitcase wobbled back and forth, and the wheels rumbled behind me. The metal handle cut into my hand as I frantically searched the mass of travelers in front of me. Finally, my colleague's faces reached out of the crowd. They waved me over and lead the way to the check-in counter. Soon we were sitting on tall barstools ordering drinks.

The second gin and tonic dispelled my panic. My body relaxed as I caught snippets of their conversation about the training week ahead. My colleagues appeared to know everything: the travel logistics, program details and the literacy jargon. Jane and Linda had leather daily planners and cell phones. They talked about school reform models, America's Choice and literacy standards. Before the trip I purchased a small, leather planner at Office Max, so I *looked* like I knew what I was doing.

On that August 6 afternoon, just three weeks after my husband's funeral, I boarded the airplane with my two new colleagues and headed across the country for our first national training together. After the long flight, a few glasses of chardonnay and a cab ride filled with chatter we arrived in D.C. We agreed to meet in the lobby after we settled into our rooms. I pulled my suitcase into the elevator and watched the numbers until the door opened. I slipped the plastic key into the slot and walked into the tiny hotel room. Everywhere I looked, John was and wasn't. Holding on to my husband's wedding band that hung on a chain around my neck, I pushed the sheer curtains open. Buildings layered, one after another, suffocated me and triggered painful memories of every city we visited during our twenty-eight years of marriage. The stiff gray building across the street reminded me of the night John died. I shook the image out of my mind, turned my back to the window and muscled my suitcase up on the bed.

With the miniature suitcase key, I unlocked the metal latch. I shuffled through the layers of clothes and dug out my eight-by-ten photo of John enclosed in a gold frame. I ran my hand along his face and kissed his cheek through the glass. I set the photo on the desk next to the guest services booklet where I could see his face when I woke up in the morning. I dug through my purse for the small plastic bottle of bourbon that I had bought on the airplane and poured myself a drink. I held the glass up and toasted John. "Welcome to D.C., sweetheart," I heard him say.

I hung my clothes in the closet and filled the dresser drawers with assorted small items. I splashed my face with cold water and headed for the lobby. After Jane introduced me to the other teachers from Saint Paul, we walked to a small restaurant across the street. Our group secured a table and ordered drinks. During our conversation over cocktails, I met another Literacy Coach. Her name was Peggy and she lived in Lakeland, a small community just a few miles down the road from me, and she attended Shepherd of the Valley, the same church I visited periodically. She was new to the program too and was not fond of flying. Amazed at how much we had in common, we immediately became friends. It was late by the time we finished dinner and headed back to the hotel. The silence of my room suffocated me. The door clicked shut. Overloaded from the day of travel, my body craved sleep. After I filled out the room service breakfast order I dialed the front desk for a wake-up call and slipped into my pajamas. The double bed—so empty.

The phone on the nightstand clanged and startled me out of a chaotic sleep filled with disjointed dreams. I crawled out of bed and squinted at the clock: 5:45. My stomach growled as I headed for the bathroom. A knock at the door followed the flush of the toilet. A second knock was accompanied with, "Room Service." I lifted the latch and clicked open the door. A young man, dressed in a gray uniform, floated into the room with a tray of plates hidden under silver covers. "Good Morning, m'ame. Where would you like your breakfast?"

I pointed to the small desk by the window. The smell of eggs and bacon filled the tiny room. I added a tip to the bill and signed my name. The man thanked me and disappeared out the door. When I uncovered the large plate of eggs, the smell gagged me, but I knew I had to eat something. I raised a fork full of scrambled eggs to my lips and choked them down. I washed the hard bacon down with gulps of orange juice and headed for the shower. The stream of water that flowed from the showerhead trickled down my back as I lathered my hair.

Refreshed from the shower, I grabbed my purse, smiled at John's picture and headed for the opening session in the main ballroom on the first floor. A woman dressed in a suit greeted me from behind a long table covered with a white cloth. She pointed to the sign-in sheet and hunted for my registration packet. She explained the nametags and meal tickets inside the envelope, then smiled and handed me a huge binder with the words "America's Choice Orientation Institute 7-11 August 2000" printed on the front.

With the thick binder under my arm, I walked into the massive room packed wall to wall with round tables and chairs. Just inside the door people crowded around a long table filled with fruit, breakfast rolls, bagels and orange juice. The aroma of coffee swirled around my head as I searched the room for my colleagues. Eventually, I spied them seated at the front of the room just inches away from the presenter's table. I wound my way through the crowd, trying not to bump anyone with my purse or binder.

Jane and Linda greeted me with a smile and pointed to the space they had saved for me. My hands shook as I pulled out the chair and slid onto the fabric cushion. The garbled voices and sound of coffee cups clanging on saucers vibrated in my head. Panic welled up inside me as a sharp pain crossed my chest. Trapped, thousands of miles away from my family, I thought I was going to die of a heart attack. Looking around the table I noticed piles of plastic wrap in the center of the table. I tore the wrapping off my binder. While I stared at the schedule for the day, the presenter enthusiastically welcomed us to "The Big Bang" training institute.

By the time our morning break arrived my head was filled with training schedules, literacy standards, analyzing student work and accountability. Overwhelmed, I excused myself and headed back to my room. I locked the door and curled up in the unmade bed. *What have I done? I can't do this.* With only a couple minutes of break left, I hauled myself out of bed, washed a white pill down and headed back to join my team. The medication helped me get through the morning. When we gathered in the dining area for lunch, I quickly ate part of my meal and returned to my room. I stretched out on the bed and covered my eyes with a hand towel. I drew in long breaths and exhaled trying to visualize fields of flowers and butterflies. The relaxation exercises calmed my body.

The afternoon sessions dragged on as I watched the minutes tick by. When 3:30 finally arrived, exhausted, I frantically packed up all my materials for a quick exit. Unfortunately, our cluster leader had other plans and informed us that we needed to stay for a "short" debriefing meeting. I sat listening to her go on and on about things I did not even understand. I was confused enough; the last thing I needed was more information.

After the meeting when everyone else went out for dinner, I headed for the hotel bar by myself. I needed to be alone. When I walked into the bar, I looked around at all the couples and people talking on their cell phones. They all seemed to be in love, excited about life. I thought maybe a cell phone would take away my sadness, connect me with friends and family. I decided to buy one when I got home. I slid onto a tall bar stool with my notebook. Every moment—alone or surrounded by strangers—filled me with anxiety. I felt like my life was going to end, and the truth was, I did not care if it did. The bartender swirled a damp terry cloth towel across the surface in front of me. "How are you tonight?" Terrible, I wanted to say. "Are you expecting others?"

"No, just me." Waiting for my husband is what I wanted to say. The bartender reminded me of a young version of my older brother Tom who had died suddenly at fifty-one. I wondered why so many of the people I loved had been ripped out of my life. I hated being a widow at fifty-three. I couldn't imagine living the rest of my life alone. As I stared at the gourmet crab salad in front of me, I wondered if I would die from all the grief. My stomach churned as I picked at the salad. I forced myself to eat the crab chunks stacked on top of the Swiss chard and curly endive lettuce. Halfway through the salad I wanted to run back to my room and go to bed. Instead, I paid the bartender, walked out the front door of the hotel and headed down the sidewalk in hopes of getting lost, shot or run over by a Fed Ex truck. No luck. Alone in my room, I held John's picture to my chest.

"I didn't want this, sweetheart. I miss you so much. The pain's so deep. I don't want to go on without you." I fell asleep with John's photo in my arms. I dreamed we were making love in a rental car by the Pacific, the ocean pounding the rocks behind us. Like the saltwater waves, we were wrapped in passion and out of control. In the darkness of the hotel room, the phone rang. The red numbers on the clock said 10:00. I shook my head. Confused, I picked up the phone. One of my new travel friends invited me to join her for a glass of wine. I declined. Even a late night glass of wine could not convince me to leave the dream behind and go down to the bar.

Each morning, the drone of the alarm clock pushed me out of bed. Sleep escaped me every night in spite of the late night cocktails with my colleagues. *Sleepless in Seattle* was a great movie. Sleepless in D.C. was a nightmare. I sat through the endless training sessions filled with more information than I could absorb, surrounded by the sound of fingers tapping on laptops and power point slides flashing across an oversized screen. We ate lunch seated around large round tables covered in white linen, drinking from iced tea glasses beaded with sweat and hearing the clanging of dishes and silverware. The constant noise agitated me. Each day I choked down half my lunch and returned to my room to cry so I could make it through the afternoon. Every morning I struggled to get up. Just showing up where I belonged took incredible energy.

Each afternoon when I returned to my room, I reached for the phone to call John to tell him about my day. Sometimes I went to the hotel bar alone and pretended John was in the restroom or caught up in a meeting.

After three days of the intense training sessions, I bottomed out. I called the 1-800 Employee Assistance line at 5:30 a.m. After several rings, a man named Carl answered. I told him I was sad, alone and that my husband had died. I told him John was all I had. I told him about my brother Tom's death, the suddenness of it all. He asked me about anxiety medication and if I was seeing a counselor. Then I told him about how I was alone when I did CPR on my husband and that the images still haunted me.

To reduce my anxiety, he suggested breathing exercises, warm baths and long walks. His calm voice soothed me for the moment. He told me to call anytime if I wanted to talk. When I hung up, I wanted the grief over, but the sun came up. I crawled out of bed and made it to the meeting in time for a cup of coffee and a blueberry muffin. The endless sessions bombarded me with power point slides filled with graphs, diagrams and bulleted lists of program "roll out" requirements. At the end of the day, confused and overwhelmed, anxiety infiltrated every nerve of my body. I had made it through another day.

That night when I went to dinner at Luigi's Italian Restaurant I searched for John everywhere along the crowded D.C. sidewalks. The animated faces of my colleagues beside me laughed, smiled and chatted on cell phones as they walked along the sidewalk in the ninety-degree heat. Their voices carried stories of children and husbands. They were so lucky. I had nothing, no one to welcome me home—only an empty house. At the restaurant our group gathered around a table by the window. The waitress scribbled our orders for cosmopolitans, martinis and white wine on her note pad. When the drinks arrived we lifted our glasses and toasted the end of another grueling day. For dinner I ordered spicy shrimp linguini and ate as much as I could.

After dinner I ordered a snifter of Courvoisier. In the midst of all the noise and garbled voices I saw John's hand wrapped around a snifter, his beautiful eyes smiling at me from across the table. As I swirled the cognac in the glass, I could smell John's cologne and feel his kiss across my lips. Before the group headed back to the hotel, I slipped into the restroom. When I came out they were gone. I did not care. I headed out the front door. Taxis and buses whizzed past me as I stood on the corner. Waiting for the light to change, I felt more connected to the bag lady dressed in red sitting alone in the bus shelter than the group that surrounded me at dinner.

Early evening shadows engulfed me as I walked the six blocks back to the hotel. The revolving door swirled me into the air-conditioned lobby, and I caught the first elevator signaling "up." Relieved to be back in my room I threw my purse on the bed, changed into my pajamas and called the front desk for a wake-up call. I lifted John's picture off the desk and hugged it. I tried some of Carl's breathing exercises, but nothing helped. I washed down a little white pill and crawled into bed.

Morning came too early. At least the week of trauma was coming to an end, one more day to get through. At lunch I picked at my spinach salad and sipped iced tea from a tall, stemmed glass with sweat beads rolling down the sides. Chatter filled the room and silverware clinked against plates. The table conversation revolved around implementation challenges, schedules and organizing materials. All I could think about was going home. I excused myself and headed back to my room. I stretched out on the bed, covered my face with a hand towel and inhaled the silence of the room. My agitated body relaxed. After splashing cold water on my face, I headed to the elevator and pushed "L." I walked through the lobby and into the chatter-filled conference room. As usual my colleagues were all seated at a round table in the front of the room. I smiled at them as I pulled out my notebook and pen. They smiled back. At the afternoon session the facilitators gave us our travel schedule. In September we were headed for Fort Worth, Texas, and two more trips after that.

Panic rippled over me. *How will I survive all these meetings and travel?* "Change your thinking," the crisis counselor had said on the phone. I didn't want to change my thinking, I wanted my life back the way it was. Part of me wanted to drop out of life, but John's voice echoed in my mind, "Keep your head up and the right path will come along." The last night of the training sessions I was on overload and ready to go home. I packed my suitcase and was in my pajamas by 9:00 when the phone rang. It was Jane, my colleague. She thought we needed some team bonding time to debrief. I hesitated, but decided that as long as we would be training together and traveling buddies, I should hike down to room 610 for a short visit.

When I knocked on the door, Jane greeted me with a smile. Linda waved at me from her chair in the corner as I wiggled past the cluttered ironing board in front of the extra double bed. I shifted her training manuals off to the side and perched myself at the edge of the bed. Jane offered me a brandy. Tempting as it was, I declined. She grabbed a pad of paper and bounced herself onto the other bed. She seemed energized and ready for a planning session.

"Can you believe this week? Oh my God, my brain is overloaded! Are you feeling the same way?"

"Oh yeah." We nodded as Jane swallowed a gulp of brandy.

"Well, I have an idea I think will help." Propped against the bed headboard, Jane handed us each a pencil and a sheet of paper. The bold typed word **Team Building** jumped off the page.

Oh great, I thought. Not one of those dumb tests. I looked at Linda sitting in the corner. As a new member of the team, I did not want to appear uncooperative, so I let Linda take the lead. I studied the questions in front of me and reconsidered the brandy offer. I poured a couple of brandy shots into the glass next to the ice bucket and wound my way back to my spot on the bed.

Jane explained how Dr. Gregorc's assessment would help us figure out our learning styles and the characteristics we each have as a team member. I stared at the groups of words that I was supposed to rank in the order based on how they described me. With my best guess, I scribbled numbers in front of the words. I don't remember if I came out as a leader, follower or team player. I didn't care. What mattered most to me was the time spent with my teammates at the end of an exhausting week of training. Sharing stories of our lives over a glass of brandy connected us as teammates and as friends.

CHAPTER 9

How Was Your Trip?

AS I PAGED through training manuals on the plane headed back to Minneapolis, I wondered how I would do everything the national trainers expected and face a week in Forth Worth at the end of September. After the endless flight from Washington, D.C., I spied Mary and Al surrounded by the crowd around the luggage carrousel. I released my grip on my suitcase and threw my arms around them. I pressed into their hugs and soaked up their warmth. Glad to be home, I sat in the back seat of their van and watched the familiar freeway lights and Mississippi River pass by in the night shadows. My shoulders finally relaxed.

When Al pulled into the driveway, the headlights flashed across the bricks on the front of the dark and empty house. I realized John would not be there to ask about my trip or to give me a hug and a kiss. I dug the house key out of my purse and pushed the door open. The security alarm screamed at me. I flipped on the light as I frantically punched the code into the keypad. Al and Mary dragged my luggage into the kitchen.

The August night was filled with the chirps of crickets and a gentle breeze. I hugged and thanked Mary and Al again as they slid into the van. Alone, I walked out on the patio and eased myself into a wrought-iron chair. Surrounded by silence and the glistening stars above, I waited for John to sit down in the chair next to me. The metal frame remained empty.

The weeks that followed the D.C. training threw me into a whirlwind of stress. The huge box of materials that I mailed back glared at me as I walked into the office on Monday morning. As I pulled each oversized binder from the cardboard box, anxiety overwhelmed me. *How would I ever read all this information and do all the training sessions? Was this job a mistake?* After several debriefing meetings with the leadership team, I pushed the binders onto the metal shelf behind my desk.

Trying to make sense out of my life, I pulled the thickest binder off the shelf and opened it to the first tabbed section "Literacy Program Overview." Each paragraph I read triggered panic. None of the notes I jotted in the margins made sense. Images of the cold, crowded D.C. conference room swirled in my head. At the end of the day, I shoved the giant binder into my rolling suitcase and trudged across the school parking lot. I pressed my head into the headrest as the car door slammed shut behind me. I drove home, along Interstate 94, in a daze. Exhausted by grief and tired of pushing myself to "move on," I crawled into bed. The sobs pounded on my chest and tears poured into the pillow. I pleaded with John to come and get me.

In late September, a 3:30 a.m. alarm rousted me out of a not so peaceful sleep. I brushed my teeth, washed down a white anxiety pill and double-checked my travel list on the bathroom counter. My colleagues and I were headed for Fort Worth, Texas, on a 7:30 a.m. flight. I paced the floor, double-checked my carry-on bag for my ticket and glanced through my itinerary. I was relieved when the headlights of Peggy's black Taurus flashed down my driveway at 5:15. Her husband dragged my luggage out of the house. I punched in the security system code and locked the door behind me. Her husband wound along the rural roads while Peggy and I talked about all the challenges ahead of us. We hoped the Fort Worth Training would give us a better sense of where we were headed.

At the airport, exhausted faces and listless bodies dozed in the gate area. I filled my time with coffee and numerous trips to the bathroom. After we boarded the plane I picked at my banana nut muffin and watched the airport disappear behind us. When we arrived at the Fort Worth airport, I followed the group through the crowds as we headed for the luggage area. They chattered about the trainings as they dragged their carryon luggage onto escalators and stopped in restrooms along the way.

Several of us rented a van. We squeezed our luggage into the back and hoisted ourselves into the rows of seats. Squashed in the back seat by the window, I stared out at the light poles and concrete barriers that whipped by as the van sped down the expressway. Constant chatter about work swirled around my head and threaded itself through the intermittent sound of the windshield wipers dragging across the windshield. My heart focused on the gray skies and the drops of rain spattering against the windows.

The vision I had in my head of Fort Worth was nothing like the experience of actually being there. I pictured our hotel with a crystal blue swimming pool, elevators that went *ding* when your floor arrived and long carpeted hallways that lead to exercise areas and meeting rooms. We wound our way along the expressway to a hotel. We sat in the van, wondering if we had read the directions wrong. Our driver reread the directions and announced, "There must be some mistake. This *can't* be it. There's no one here." The young woman wearing the baseball cap next to me threw her head back and laughed, "Yup, this is it. The sign says 'Hidden Green Inn.'"

The two floors of interconnected rooms each with a door to the outside stretched from one corner of the parking lot to the other. The hotel looked like a senior citizen residence. The deserted lobby smothered me as I walked toward the front desk with Jane and Linda. After we checked in, I dragged my suitcase up two flights of wooden stairs to my room. The dark, depressing room matched my mood and felt like a tomb even with the drapes pulled open. I grabbed my key and hiked down the walkway to Jane's room. With a quick phone call Jane made fast plans to relocate to the Hawthorne Suites next door. With our luggage in hand, we headed for the lobby. Linda walked up to the receptionist and told her we were checking out. Without a second thought the woman took our keys and canceled our reservation. After we settled into our new rooms, we headed to Pappasito's Cantina for dinner and drinks. Starving, I consumed a basket of chips and a dish of salsa. By the time my fajitas arrived I was full, but I consumed the tortillas anyway. Every night after the endless sessions we searched out a new place for dinner. One night after dinner at a Tex-Mex restaurant we returned to the hotel for some team bonding time. With a cheap bottle of brandy and a bucket of ice we laughed, watched the Olympics and played the "truth and lie" game, which I lost.

The next day, during our training sessions, people staying at the Hidden Green told us they had trouble sleeping because of the cockroaches crawling across their pillows. We had made the right decision to change hotels. At the end of the week Linda, Jane and our principal decided we needed to celebrate surviving the intense week of training. The four of us piled into the rental car and headed for Billy Bob's, "The World's Largest Honky Tonk." As our principal drove, we talked about the training sessions. We wondered how we would ever get teachers in our building to change their teaching practices and believe that our students would meet the high national literacy standards.

When we pulled into the parking lot I stared at the lighted TEXAS sign on top of the huge beige building in front of us. The smell of manure and the distant sound of honky tonk music filled the air as we strolled through the parking lot. The music combined with the soft green, yellow and amber lights surrounding the entrance lifted my spirits. Inside, the click of pool balls, slot machine bells and laughter swirled around me. One part of me wanted to run back to the car, the other wanted Billy Bob's honky-tonk energy to swallow me up. I followed my team through the crowded room, past the wall filled with photos of Willie Nelson, Waylon Jennings and other famous county western singers. We headed toward the neon "Coors" and "Lone Star" beer signs above the saloon's bar. With a bottle of "Lone Star" in my hand, I wandered over to the dance floor. I watched as couples dressed in tight jeans and cowboy boots twirled and two-stepped to the rhythm of the guitars and fiddles on stage.

Several single guys in cowboy hats leaned on the timber railing, tapping their feet to the music. I lifted my beer to my lips and took a long, slow draw. I stared at my wedding ring, slipped it off my finger and dropped my twenty-eight years of marriage into my purse. I watched the men on the dance floor and tried to imagine being married to them. "Too heavy. He smokes. Too old. Great dancer." I was relieved when Jane's face appeared in the crowd. She waved me over and we headed across the room and joined the others.

The four of us stopped at a photo area where a couple laughed hysterically as they slid down from the back of a black and white fake bull. Within minutes Jane and Linda convinced us that "riding a bull" was just what we needed after the grueling week of training. Not wanting to disappoint my team I pulled on a pair of red, fringed chaps, tied a blue bandana around my neck and pushed a black hat onto my head. I climbed onto the bull, straddled his head and held onto its horn. With the four of us lined up we raised our hands into the air. The pretend crowd roared behind us and the fake bull seemed to come to life. Smiles covered our faces as the photographer snapped the camera.

Before we left, I stopped in the restroom. While drying my hands I remembered my wedding ring in my purse and decided I was not ready to be single. I dug through my purse, but could not find the ring. Panic rolled over me. *Why did I take it off? What was I thinking?* I set my shoulder bag on the wet counter and pulled everything out of my purse one piece at a time. Then I remembered before the bull photo I had zipped the ring into my wallet. I pulled the ring out of the coin section and slipped it back on my thin finger. I kissed the diamonds, reloaded my purse and joined my friends at the front door.

♪♪♪♫

The Fort Worth national training provided our team with tons of literacy information, but minimal preparation for the challenges ahead of us as "agents of change." Initially, our after-school training sessions were often met with crossed arms and skepticism. Standing next to the overhead, I tried to draw energy from the few friendly faces sprinkled through the crowd. New to the building, I wanted to believe that our students' test scores would improve. Yet, with 90 percent of the students on free or reduced lunches and more than a dozen languages spoken in the building, I had my doubts. Improvement seemed impossible. Daily statements from staff that started with "Yes, but . . ." fueled my doubts, added to my stress and made me question my decision to leave my predictable fifth-grade classroom.

As coaches, Linda, Jane and I spent our days helping teachers implement Writer's Workshop in their classrooms. We carried our training manuals in plastic totes and chart paper from room to room. We modeled lessons and met with teachers in small groups before and after school hoping they would embrace the change and believe our students could write for forty minutes a day. The pressure from the state and district to improve our test scores was a constant stress. Coupled with the principal's decision to reduce the building-wide recess time in order to increase the amount of instructional time, the change was a tough sell.

A month after the Fort Worth training trip at one of our leadership meetings, someone suggested we present at the national conference in Jacksonville, Florida, in January. I wondered what they were thinking. With our minimal expertise and binders still in their shrink wrap, how could we possibly explain to a room filled with teachers, administrators and national literacy experts how to successfully implement change in their buildings? But inspired by a week in Jacksonville in January away from the bitter cold Minnesota weather, we were headed for sunny Florida.

During the weeks that followed, Linda, Jane and I worked on the presentation. We videotaped Writer's Workshops where students shared their thoughts about writing and read their work in front of the camera. We interviewed teachers and our music specialist even wrote a song, "Patience," to go with our video. On the day we recorded the song the music teacher handed us percussion instruments. As she sang and strummed her guitar, Jane rattled the maracas while

I shook a cabasa hoping the rhythm of the wood cylinder wrapped in a steel ball chain occasionally matched a beat. We looked more like tourists in a Cancun bar after several shots of tequila than like literacy coaches.

Between videotaping students, presenting lessons in classrooms and facilitating staff trainings before and after school, I counted the days until Christmas vacation. The week before break with our presentation video finished, Jane, Linda and I gathered around a table in our office to preview it. The students' proud faces beamed as they read their writing. In their interviews, teachers admitted they were skeptical about Writer's Workshop at first, but were amazed at how much the students enjoyed writing. Their enthusiasm and positive comments brought tears to my eyes. In spite of all the challenges we faced, I realized we were touching the lives of our students and inspiring change in our building. During the long drive home on the snow-covered roads, images from the video flashed through my head. I wanted to share my excitement and the proud smiles on our students' faces with John. When the Probe pushed through the drift-filled driveway and the garage door slammed shut behind me, only the dark house and screaming security system welcomed me home.

CHAPTER 10

Winter Woes

DRESSED IN MY snow pants, ski jacket, hat, hiking boots and oversized mittens, I headed for the garage. I studied the red, eight horsepower Murray snowblower nestled between the lawn mower and garden cart on the far side of the garage. I pulled off my mittens. My breath hung in the air as I unscrewed the blower's gas cap. I poured gas into the fuel tank and plugged the electric start chord into the wall. I reread the directions on the blower several times before I adjusted the throttle, set the choke, pumped the primer and pushed the start button.

After groaning and sputtering, the sweet sound of the Briggs and Stratton motor roared to life. "Hallelujah! Thank God!" I shouted. Fumes from the over rich fuel mixture permeated the air as I studied the six gear choices and shifted into second. I pulled my mittens over my tingling fingers and muscled the blower out into the drifts. I engaged the auger lever. The Murray and I were off to clear the driveway.

Under the stars, with only the rumble of the snowblower for company, I walked the length of the endless driveway alone; back and forth. With each step the auger churned through the resistant, hard-packed drifts, pulling the snow into the twenty-four-inch scoop. The snow rolled through the internal guts of the blower and blasted out the chute. Invisible ice crystals carried by the wind stung my cheeks.

I struggled to push the heavy metal blower through the packed snow, but the crisp Minnesota air energized me and kept me going.

With the snowblower back in the garage, I grabbed the shovel off the wall and headed for the deck. The lights on the deck glowed in the darkness and sparked memories of our first Christmas in our one bedroom apartment in Saint Paul. The shovel scraped across the cedar deck while my mind floated back to 1972. After purchasing a tree from a local lot, we tied it to the top of our beige Volkswagen Beetle and headed back to our apartment on McKnight Road on the east side of Saint Paul. Our third-floor apartment presented quite the challenge. The caretaker frowned upon residents dragging Christmas trees into the elevator and down hallways. John drove the Volkswagen around to the back of the complex and parked it on the street below our apartment. Standing on the balcony, I threw one end of a long rope down to John. He tied the rope to the trunk of the tree.

A few minutes later, standing side by side, we pulled together as the tree inched closer and closer to our balcony. We laughed as we rolled the bundle of green over the railing. The sharp needles scraped against our faces as we hauled the tree into the living room through our sliding glass door, embedding needles in the plush carpet. While the tree warmed up, John sat on the floor and tested the lights while I relaxed on the couch, munching chips and sipping my holiday cheer. That evening, we decorated our first tree with the cheap Shiny Brite ornaments we purchased for $1.59 a box at the local Target. I had enjoyed shopping at Target ever since the first store opened in Roseville, Minnesota in 1962. Before going to bed, we poured a short nightcap. In the glow of the Christmas tree lights, we snuggled together on the couch. We talked about the wonderful evening and looked forward to all the Christmases ahead of us.

The mournful sound of coyotes howling in the darkness crashed through my memories and pulled me back to the deck. Shivering and alone, I dumped the last scoop of snow over the deck railing and hung the shovel back in the garage. Exhausted, I sat on a plastic chair under the December stars and stared into the void beyond the deck. My ski jacket reeked of snowblower fumes, and my sweat-soaked hair clung to my cheeks as I tried to imagine the holidays without John. That night I decided to skip Christmas: no cards, no tree, no cookies.

🎵🎵🎵🎵

A few days before Christmas break, after another long drive home from work, I pushed open the back door. The kitchen's warmth covered my cold cheeks. Relieved to be home, I stomped the snow off my boots and hung up my coat. The red light flashed on the answering machine, the only sign of activity in the empty house. Even though eight months had passed since John's first time in the intensive care unit, the red light on the answering machine still triggered waves of panic through my body. Ignoring the amber light, I poured myself a glass of wine and flipped through the mail on the counter, just Christmas cards and junk mail, nothing important. I stared at the answering machine. Then tapped the message button.

"Hi, Di, just wondering how your drive was with all the snow. Call me when you get home. Love you, bye."

Since John's first stay in the hospital, my sister Mary had been my strongest supporter. Standing in the kitchen I looked at the clock: 6:15. I figured they would be eating dinner and planned to call them later. Except for the whirr of the refrigerator and the hum of the furnace, silence filled the house. I wandered from room to room, flipping on lights to keep myself company. For a few minutes, I stood by the living room window and studied the snowdrifts below. My eyes landed on a bulging shape nestled in the snow by the sliding glass door. At first I thought it might be a deer bedded down for the night. I tapped on the window, but the shape did not move.

My heart raced as I tiptoed down the stairs to the lower level to get a better look. A tree; it was a Christmas tree nestled on the edge of the solid snowdrift. *That's strange, how did that get there?* Puzzled, I headed back upstairs, refilled my wineglass, picked up the phone and dialed my sister's number.

After a few rings Mary answered, "Hello, Di. Isn't this snow terrible? I thought about you while I drove home. I was worried about you. How was your drive?"

"Nerve wracking. The freeway was pure ice and tons of tail lights. I got off before the river exit, but the drifted back roads were worse. The drive took forever. When I got home I found a Christmas tree outside the lower level window. I have no idea where it came from."

"That's interesting. Must be a sign that you should celebrate Christmas. John would want you to."

"I know, but Mary, it's so hard. Just the thought of putting up a tree by myself and decorating it makes me miss him even more. We put up a tree every year. I can't do it, I just can't."

"Diane, it's been six months. You have to move on, get back into life. You can't go on this way. I'll drive down. We can decorate it together. How does that sound?"

"I don't know. It's such a long drive for you and the weather is so bad. Your family needs you."

"I want to help, Di. We can go out for dinner first. How about Friday night? We wouldn't have to get up for work on Saturday." I stared at my reflection in the window, wishing John were outside shoveling in the shadows, but only drifts of snow and my own reflection stared back, a grim reminder of my lonely life.

"Well, if you want to drive all the way down here, Friday would work. But really, Mary, you don't have to. If I decide to put up the tree, I can do it alone."

"Don't do it alone, Di. The kids are old enough to stay home without me for an hour after school. They will be fine until Al gets home at four-thirty. Let's plan on four-thirty, Friday. That'll give us time to go out for dinner before we decorate. Can you be home from work by then?"

I thought for a moment before I answered, "I think so, unless the weather gets bad. I will call you on my cell phone before I leave school. I should be home by four-fifteen. Thanks, Mary, I didn't want it this way."

"I know, Di. You'll get through this. You're strong. I'm proud of you. See you Friday. Hang in there. I love you."

"I love you too, Mary. Give Al and the kids a hug for me."

I clicked off the phone and studied the white minilights strung along the deck railing. I remembered the frigid November day, when, trying to keep my life the way it was, I had hung the lights just like John and I had done so for the last several years. That day, the bitter cold burned my fingers as I draped the evergreen garland along the railing and secured the white minilights with plastic electrical straps. When the automatic timer flipped the lights on that night, I had stood by the window and sobbed. Now, in the December darkness, the sparkles welcomed me home each night as I turned the Probe into the snow-covered driveway. The lights inspired me to keep struggling forward. At the same time the glow signaled to others that I was "moving on," which was a lie.

The ring of the telephone startled me and drew me back to the kitchen. My neighbor's named appeared on the caller ID. The minute I picked up the phone he asked if I had found the tree he had left for me. I told him what a surprise it was and asked how much he wanted for it. He refused to take any money. Before hanging up, I thanked him for his thoughtfulness. In spite of the Christmas cards arriving in my mailbox, I struggled to find joy in the holiday season ahead. I hoped the tree trimming night with my sister would magically inspire a joyful spirit within me. That July day when friends and family prayed at John's graveside, Christmas had seemed so far away. Six months later the thought of spending the holiday alone created a hollow feeling in my heart. I wandered through the empty house, talking to myself and searching for John.

With winter break as my incentive, I tried my best to keep going, but knew I couldn't keep struggling every day at work, trying to keep my emotions in check. In hopes of an instant answer to my pain, I called the doctor, the same one who had treated John. He just happened to have an opening early the next morning. When I arrived the nurse greeted me with a hug. She studied the scale as the numbers appeared on the monitor and noticed I had lost ten pounds since my last visit. She led me into the examination room and checked my

73

blood pressure. A few minutes later the doctor bustled through the door. He told me again how sorry he was about John. I broke into tears. He tried to console me as he pressed his stethoscope against my boney chest. Concerned about my weight loss and borderline high blood pressure he wrote me a prescription for Paxil, assuring me the medication would help. When I arrived at work, I washed the first pill down praying it would take the pain away.

On Thursday after work, with the tree mystery solved and my sister's promise to help me decorate it, I decided to get the tree in the stand and drag it into the house so it would be ready to decorate on Friday when she arrived. I dug through the storage area under the basement steps where we stored the Christmas decorations. I stooped low enough to reach the small tree stand at the very back of the cramped space. I figured this tree was so small that the smallest stand would work, plus it was closer to the front. I grabbed the metal rim and started to back out of the space. I raised my head too fast and clunked it on a two-by-four. "Damn! That hurt. I hate doing this alone." I rubbed my head and crouched even lower and backed out with the metal tree stand in hand. I unlocked the sliding glass door and set the stand by the window. Bundled up in my down jacket, boots and gloves I headed for the garage to get the bow saw and pruning shears.

The December darkness replaced the last few flecks of daylight. Snowdrifts covered the well-worn path through the snow to the back of the house. The crisp winter air filled the evening with silence. I pulled my gloves off and wrapped my left hand around the skinny trunk of the tree to steady it. The cold bit my face as the salty taste of tears lingered on my lips. Puffs of my breath lingered in the darkness.

I steadied the bow saw an inch above the bottom of the tree trunk. I pushed the saw back and forth for three strokes. Through my icy tears I watched as the bottom chunk of the tiny balsam tree dropped onto the snow. I loosened the three metal bolts on the bottom of the stand and then eased the stand over the stump of the trunk. My fingers tingled as the stand caught on the two small pine branches above the new cut. "Crap, I have to clip a few more branches off."

I grabbed the frigid pruning sheers off the hard snow. After clipping a few strategic branches off the bottom, I shoved the metal prongs on the stand into the base of the trunk. With my sticky, sap-covered fingers, I tightened the bolts as best as I could and stood the tree upright. Even in the stand the balsam was shorter than I was. "Oh well, it was a gift and the decorations will help." I slid the heavy glass door open, grabbed the tree by the trunk and lifted it into the family room.

With the December cold locked outside I took off my down jacket and studied the tiny pine. *Hmmm, it's crooked, needs to go a little to the left.* I crawled under the tree and slowly loosened a bolt on the left, then gently pulled the trunk toward me and tightened the bolt on the opposite side. I wished John was there to help. He always adjusted the stand while I held the trunk and guided him. After I wiggled out from under the tree, I brushed the pine needles from my hair. Exhausted, I collapsed on the couch and stared at the pathetic shape in front of me. The aroma of pine pitch triggered memories of our Christmases together.

My tears mingled with the pine fragrance, the tree a blur in front of me. The clock we bought in Scotland stared at me and yelled, "It's 10:00 p.m. Get to bed. You have to go to work tomorrow!" *How could it be that late?* Every project took so much longer now that I was alone. The only sounds I heard in the family room were the clock's ticking and the pine needles landing on the carpet. Instead of heading upstairs to my lonely bedroom I rewarded my successful tree project with a glass of port. I sipped the warm ruby wine hoping it would replace the clock's ticking with the sound of John's voice. I knew it was late, and I had an early meeting. I didn't care.

CHAPTER 11

First Christmas

AS PROMISED, MY sister arrived Friday afternoon to help with the tree trimming. The last few glimpses of daylight reflected off her car as she pulled into the driveway and crawled out with a shopping bag in her hand. A burst of December air followed her through the back door and snowflakes clung to the wool scarf around her neck. I wrapped her in a hug. Happy to see her, I held her bag as she pulled off her coat and dropped her boots by the door. She handed me a holiday tin. Lifting the cover, I discovered layers of gorgeous Christmas cookies nestled in wax paper that she and the kids had made the night before. She thought they would come in handy if I had company. *Company, I doubted that.* I thanked her, thinking I could always take them to work and put them in the staff room.

Before starting our tree-trimming project, we climbed into Mary's car and drove down the winding road to "downtown" Afton. With a total township population of just over twenty-five hundred people, Afton's downtown consisted of a few quaint shops and a post office nestled together at the edge of the scenic St. Croix River. The Catfish was the only restaurant in the tiny town open in the winter. For some odd reason Afton managed to stay locked in the past while the surrounding areas sprouted malls, fast food restaurants and gas stations. Snuggled against the shore of the scenic St. Croix River, the tiny town provided a tranquil setting to relax and enjoy nature. The red bows and evergreen garland wrapped around the gaslights along the quiet street looked like a winter scene out of a Charles Dickens's story.

Shivering, we slid into a booth and pulled off our gloves. I rubbed my hands together and blew on my fingers. The waitress arrived with two ice waters and menus. After reciting the specials and taking drink orders, she headed back to the kitchen.

"Well, how hungry are you?" Mary asked as she studied the menu. I had not eaten much all day.

"Not very."

"You really need to eat better, Di. You don't want to get sick." *I WAS sick.* Sick of eating alone, sick of sleeping in a cold bed without John and sick of the anxiety that plagued me. I wanted my life back the way it was. Going on alone sucked. Eating was not the problem, living the rest of my life alone was. The oversized glass of chardonnay the waitress set in front of me tickled my lips and the tart aroma filled my nostrils while we waited for our food. By the time the waitress delivered our order, half the wine had disappeared out of my glass. I picked at the cheeseburger and fries in the plastic basket as I watched my sister nibble away at her dinner salad. After choking down only half of the cheeseburger and a few fries, I knew I couldn't finish my meal. I leaned away from the table and dug my wallet out of my purse.

I boxed my leftover burger, pickle and fries, even though I'd probably throw it out. Outside, our breath hung in the air as we crawled into the frigid car and headed home along the dark, twisting road, hoping a deer wouldn't leap out of the brush along the road. The lights on the deck greeted us as we drove into the driveway. With our boots off and coats draped over the chairs, we headed downstairs. I flipped on the light and Mary smiled.

"What a cute little tree. I love the smell." She walked around it and studied it from different angles while I crawled into the storage area under the steps and pulled out the plastic containers filled with decorations John and I had collected over our twenty-eight years of marriage. This time I remembered to keep my head tucked down so I would not wallop it on the sloped ceiling. One by one, I pushed the blue plastic containers into the family room. I pried the top off of the bin labeled "lights and family decorations." Opening the lid released every Christmas John and I had shared together.

"I can't do this, Mary. It's too hard."

"We don't have to trim the tree if you don't want to." I looked at the tree and thought about all the energy I had already invested in getting the tree in the stand. I figured it was too late to stop.

"Let's keep going. Maybe once it's decorated it'll put me in the Christmas spirit." Mary reached into the box and pulled out the strings of multicolored minilights.

We figured two strings would be more than enough. As we stepped around the tree, my sister draped the lights up and down the branches. The tree was so small that we decided to hang the lights and decorations mostly on the front side of the tiny tree. Besides, no one except the deer could see the back of the tree. With the lights draped on the branches, we hung the silver and blue balls John and I had purchased at Target for our first Christmas. Then we each took the family ornaments one at time and strategically placed them in safe places on the tree. The oldest family ornament was a tarnished gold ball laced with tiny antique beads that our parents had purchased for their first Christmas during World War II.

Every year this special ornament had received the sturdiest branch. I gently hooked it on a thick branch at the top of the tree next to Angie, The Christmas Tree Angel, another antique that had been at the top of our family's tree forever. As I stared at the old ornaments I could see my siblings and me sitting on the living room floor at my parents' home, opening presents one by one with Christmas music playing on the record player and reused wrapping paper and ribbons scattered all over the floor.

With all the decorations dangling from the branches and the gold garland in place, I filled the small metal stand with water and carefully arranged the new tree skirt with some gold stitching and the fringe along the edge my sister had made for me.

"Mary, the new tree skirt is perfect."

"I had some of that satin material left over from a dress I made and figured it would make a great tree skirt. Well, should we turn off the lights and see how the tree looks?" I walked over to the polished brass light switch and pushed the light off as Mary clicked the tree lights on. The tiny tree garnished with gold garland sparkled in front of the window.

"Oh, it's beautiful." I tried to swallow my tears, but the tiny drop-lets filled my eyes and rolled down my cheeks. "Thanks, Mary. I appreciate all you've done for me. I wouldn't have made it this far without you." She told me I was a strong woman and that John would be proud of me. Standing in the kitchen, Mary pulled on her snow boots and coat. We wrapped each other up in a long hug. Before leaving she suggested I join them for Christmas Eve. Not wanting to impose any more than I already had, I told her I would watch the weather forecast and think about it.

I stood by the kitchen window and watched the Toyota's taillights disappear into the winter darkness. Except for the subtle whir of the furnace fan, solitude crept through the house. I headed back downstairs to finish putting up a few decorations. I dug through the box with the Santas and angels. I pulled out the wooden Christmas plate my mother painted years ago when I was in kindergarten. I eased the plastic bag off and cradled the plate in my hands and studied the fifty-year-old painting of our family. My father led the group with a wreath in his hand. My mother walked behind him wearing a bulky blue coat and fancy hat. My older brother, Tom, followed behind her carrying a present while I tagged along at the end, a tiny, dark-haired girl, dressed in a brown coat with my hands tucked in a white fur muff. On the rim of the plate in her fancy script my mother lettered "MERRY CHRISTMAS."

With the plate cradled in my hands, memories of my family triggered a pain inside me. I ran my hand along the smooth border of the plate and then stroked the brushed images of my smiling family walking together. Even though there were four people on the plate, I only saw myself walking at the end of the line. I was the only one left from that Merry Christmas image.

My parents had died a year apart when they were in their sixties, and my brother Tom, two years older than me, had died suddenly at fifty-one just four years before John. After losing so many people in my life, surviving the loss of my husband seemed impossible. I hung the plate on the wall. In memory of my parents and brother, I poured a glass of wine and grabbed a thumbprint cookie from my sister's container. A sudden CRASH echoed up the stairwell.

"What was that?" I grabbed my wine and ran downstairs. The Christmas tree was on the floor with its lights still glowing. Shattered ornaments covered the white carpet.

"Oh God, I can't take this anymore!" I screamed as my eyes darted from the tree to the ornaments and landed on the puddle of water soaking into the carpet. "I can't believe this. Everything I try to do fails. I hate this, John. Please, come and get me."

I sat on the bottom step in the glow of the tumbled tree. I felt John's touch, his smile and heard his laugh. Our conversations over candlelight meals reeled through my head. The sharp ring of the phone drew me back to the family room and the mess. Instead of running up the steps, I let the machine pick up the message. The message from my sister filtered down the stairwell. "Hi, Diane. Hope you're enjoying the tree. Talk to you later." When the machine clicked off, I swallowed a huge gulp of wine.

Yeah, right, enjoying the tree, I thought. All I wanted to do was go to bed, but I knew I could not leave the mess until morning. I pushed myself off the step, flipped on the light and walked over to the tree. I unplugged the lights and lifted the tree upright. As I walked around the tree I realized only a few of the cheap bulbs and the tree top ornament were broken. All the other ornaments were still in place and unharmed. My eyes darted to the top of the tree where the blue Christmas angel hung next to the antique family beaded ornament. I could not believe the old World War II family ornament was unharmed and still dangling on the sturdy branch beside the angel.

After apologizing to God for screaming, I soaked up the puddle of water with a hand towel and picked up the fragments of shiny metal balls off the floor. With the tree upright in its stand, I realized that the weight of all the lights and ornaments on the front side had unbalanced the tree and caused it to fall. Taking off all the decorations and starting over was my only option. It was almost midnight by the time I finished undecorating the miniature balsam and strategically rehanging all the lights and ornaments. I draped the gold garland on the limbs, making sure I threaded it along the branches on the backside. With all the boxes pushed back into the storage area, I remembered the cookie on the counter in the kitchen. I decided it would be a great way to celebrate my accomplishment.

When I walked into the kitchen the red light on the answering machine blinked at me. I jotted "Call Mary" on the pad by the phone and grabbed two frosted star cookies. With the cookies in hand I strolled back downstairs, switched off the lights and admired the tree as I relaxed on the sectional. In the silence John's voice whispered, "Good job, sweetheart. I'm proud of you."

After the tree disaster, for the first time in weeks, I fell into a solid sleep filled with disjointed dreams of John. In one dream he sat alone on a bench at the Apple Orchard Golf Course. Dressed in a yellow golf shirt, khaki cotton slacks and his blue Pebble Beach visor. With a smile on his face he leaned back on the bench, waiting to tee up. Later, we sat across from each other at a table for two, covered with white linen. A single tea light glowed between us. Suddenly, John stood up and walked away. I ran out of the restaurant, down streets and alleys in the dark, but could not find him. I screamed his name into the shadowed doorways but only silence answered. Terrified, I opened my eyes and the sun poked through the edge of the bedroom shades. When I realized it was just a dream my racing pulse slowed. I rolled over and touched the empty space next to me.

The phone blared at me from the nightstand. I grabbed the handset and glanced at the caller ID. It was my sister. Worried why I hadn't returned her call, I explained how the tree fell over and it was too late to call by the time I cleaned up the mess and redecorated the tree. Again she suggested I join them for Christmas. I finally gave in. Like the weekends, the winter days were too short. Between phone calls, chores and errands, daylight faded into dusk. Saturday melted into Sunday. Sadness settled over the house as soon as the sun disappeared. Sunday night after I finished my microwave meal, I bundled up in ski clothes and went outside. I eased myself into the wrought iron rocking chair on the snow-covered patio and watched clouds of my breath disappear into the darkness.

Alone under the stars I prayed that God would bring John back. I wondered if God was even listening anymore. I searched the skies for some sign; I believed John was up there somewhere. The cold finally filtered through my nylon ski pants and drove me into the warmth of the house. After a hot bath I pulled on my sweats, took a pill and crawled into bed. For once sleep came easily. The drive into school took two hours. Tempted to turn around and go home, I stuck with the traffic crawling across town. I felt woozy and faint. By lunchtime I was not sure I would make it through the last day before winter break, but the hugs and smiles from the students carried me through to dismissal.

On Christmas Eve day, I stuffed my sweats into an overnight bag, along with John's picture, and headed to my sister's. Christmas songs whirled through the car as I drove north along County Road 18. As I passed through Stillwater, couples holding hands and a few last- minute shoppers shuffled along the sidewalks, gazing into store windows. The holiday music and lonely drive threw me into a panic. I gripped the steering wheel and searched for a place on the scenic road to turn around. I didn't want to worry my sister, so I kept driving. To calm myself, I shut off the radio and pushed an Indian flute music tape into the cassette player. Giant pine trees and snow drifts flashed by the windows. I forced myself to focus on the gray road ahead while the gentle flute music calmed me.

Standing in the entryway, I set my shopping bag of gifts on the floor and stomped the snow off my boots. Mary sprinted up the steps and hugged me. She squashed my coat into the hall closet. When I walked down the steps into the living room more hugs and Merry Christmases greeted me. My friend Paula jumped up from the couch, wrapped her arms around me and whispered, "Glad you came."

After dinner, laughter and holiday music filled the room. With amber logs glowing in the fireplace, we toasted family and friends. Like a bandage over a fresh wound, the festive mood hid my pain while we sat around the tree, sipped our drinks and took turns opening gifts. My brother-in-law snapped photos of Paula, Mary and me sitting on the hearth. Wearing a black sweater and the silver seagull necklace John bought me at our favorite art gallery on the North Shore of Lake Superior, I stared at the camera and tried to smile. When the flash went off my brother-in-law joked, "Ah, come on girls, give me a smile."

With the fire crackling behind us, I pushed a fake smile across my face as the flash went off. After everyone left we picked up the scraps of wrapping paper, the empty beverage glasses and said goodnight. Standing alone in my niece's bedroom I realized I had forgotten to take my antidepressant pill. After brushing my teeth, I washed the pill down with a glass of water, clicked the bedroom door closed, and pulled John's photo out of my travel bag. Dressed in my sweats I lay on the bed, stroking his face with my finger . . . .

Christmas morning arrived with partly cloudy skies and a glimmer of sunshine. In our pajamas, we sipped coffee and opened more presents. Halfway through the morning, I crashed. I wanted to go home. The smell of ham roasting in the oven nauseated me. Mary insisted I stay for dinner. To calm the grief rumbling inside me, I walked upstairs to the master bedroom and curled up on the bed. I took deep breaths, determined to make the pain go away. Nothing helped. Mary appeared at the door with an afghan in her arms. She smoothed the handmade throw over me and asked if I was hungry. I shook my head. She rubbed my arm and closed the door behind her.

CHAPTER **12**

Holiday Angels

ARRIVING HOME, EXHAUSTED from the long drive and Elvis Presley's "Blue Christmas" lyrics playing incessantly on the car radio, I crawled into our cold, lonely bed. I tried blocking out Elvis's melancholy voice, but it refused to leave. In the morning, after a restless sleep, I raised the pleated bedroom shades. Bright December sunshine poured into the bedroom. The blue sky, a refreshing break from the string of gray Minnesota winter days, lifted my heart.

A winter chill covered the house. I checked the thermostat in the hallway. Shivering, I turned the dial up from sixty-five to sixty-eight. The furnace motor clicked on. In the kitchen I spooned the coffee grounds into the brewing basket, filled the reservoir with twelve cups of water and clicked on the switch. The pot gurgled as I flipped through three days of mail piled on the counter. I filled my favorite cup with the fresh brewed coffee and wandered downstairs to check on the tree. Relieved to see the evergreen still upright, I clicked the minilights on and curled up in the corner of the sectional.

With a decorated tree and my sister's cookies, I decided to invite a few people over during the holidays. I thought maybe keeping some of the traditions the same would help. At first I was excited about company. I already had lights up on the deck railing and a few scattered in the rose bushes along the front of the house. I even had a wreath and four memorial ice candles outside the front window that glowed at night in memory of John, my brother and my parents. I decided to call John's mom, his brother and my brother Mike to invite them over for our traditional "goofy gift" night.

I perused the scant food supply in my refrigerator and cabinets. If company was coming, I knew I had to drive into town for groceries and pick up a few items at Fleet Farm. I pulled off my sweats and layered on a T-shirt, turtleneck, a heavy sweater, tights and a pair of well-worn jeans. At Fleet Farm I searched for John in the hardware aisles, hoping to find him reading labels on paint cans or hunting down materials for one of our home improvement projects.

At the grocery store my eyes darted from shelf to shelf. Carts piled with groceries and screaming children filled the aisles. Halfway through the store, I wanted to abandon my cart and run out the door. Pushing images of a dead husband out of my mind, I gripped the red cart handle and wound my way through the frozen food department. I grabbed a few frozen dinners and a couple pizzas, then headed for the check out lane. Even the *beep-beep* of the cashier's scanner agitated me as I waited in line. Finally, I unloaded my groceries on the conveyor belt and handed the cashier my coupons. After I nestled the last few items into the top of the grocery bags, I rolled the cart out the door and into the parking lot.

Over the next few days I touched up the house and wrapped the "goofy gifts," inexpensive items I purchased at Fleet Farm. Friends called to see how I was doing; some of their voices carried support, others triggered my loss. The sound of a man's voice at the end of the phone churned up memories of John and reminded me that my life would never be the same. The aroma of lasagna baking in the oven filled the air as Mike drove into the driveway. Glad he arrived first, I squeezed him in a long hug. A few minutes later John's brother and eighty-seven-year-old mother shuffled their way along the snow-glazed driveway to the back door. Ethel handed me a shopping bag filled their "goofy gifts" and a pan of homemade rolls.

After I piled the coats on the bed in the guest bedroom, I poured drinks and we headed downstairs. Everyone loved the tree and enjoyed the tree disaster story. Sitting on the couch, dressed in her turquoise sweater and green slacks, Ethel stared at the tree. We all felt John's absence. Ethel continued to maintain her belief that God had His reason for taking John, but in her distant gaze I could feel her emptiness and the loss of her youngest son. After our simple lasagna dinner, we opened our "goofy gifts." Ethel peeled tissue paper off cans of soup while John's brother held up a bag of cashews for the camera. I waited until last to pass out the little memory gifts of John. I gave Ethel a small, carved box where John stored pennies, and his brother, having the same initials as John, enjoyed the tie tack with "JWH" engraved on it. Mike unwrapped an old pocketknife of John's and rolled it around in his hand, admiring it from different angles. Around 8:30 everyone packed up to leave. We stood in the kitchen and talked about John and how we missed him. After hugs all around, they eased their cars out of the driveway and the red taillights disappeared.

I stood alone in the kitchen, waving, even though I knew they couldn't see me. Silence rolled across the kitchen counters and din- ing room table. All I could hear was the hum of the furnace and the beat of my own heart. I wound down the staircase to the lower level, smoothed out the scraps of festive wrapping paper and gathered the reused green and red bows. I dumped pieces of walnut shells into the wastebasket and collected the drink glasses hidden among the empty gift boxes and tissue paper on the coffee table. With the Christmas clutter under control, I snuggled into the sectional and propped my feet up on the coffee table. Staring at the blue angel at the top of the tree, I told John how much we missed him, then asked him to tell me what to do about our traditional New Year's Eve get together with friends.

John and I had celebrated New Year's Eve with the same group of people for twenty-eight years. Our tradition started our first New Year's Eve together, before we were married. A close friend of John's invited us to a party at their apartment in Brooklyn Center, a suburb of Minneapolis. We snacked on cocktail wieners and bacon-wrapped water chestnuts while we drank our favorite cocktails filled with rum, scotch or bourbon. A few minutes before midnight, we turned on the television to watch Dick Clark in Times Square and welcomed the New Year with champagne, hugs and kisses

Eventually, the group decided meeting at a restaurant made more sense. With John gone, the thought of driving across town alone to meet our friends unnerved me. A few days before our annual New Year's Eve get together, I called John's best friend, whom he had known since high school. The familiar voice answered with a cheery hello. When I told him I would not be joining them for New Year's Eve, there was a pause at the end line. When he tried to talk me into coming, I insisted it was too far to drive, too cold, too slippery. He seemed to understand. Through tears I told him that I would love to have all of them out to the house for a visit. He thought that was a good idea and wished me a happy new year. After I hung up the phone, I stood by the counter and cried. I hated letting my friends down, but knew I couldn't ring in 2001 alone.

Instead of an overpriced dinner at an upscale restaurant, I spent New Year's Eve tromping through the deep snow in the yard on my cross-country skis. I could not believe how much my legs ached from such a short time in the snow. *How did I get so out of shape?* Grieving John's death and the stress of my new job had consumed every ounce of my energy. I couldn't remember the last time I did a sit-up or used the treadmill. Not ready to go inside, I propped my cross-country skis against the wall in the garage and dug out our minigrill. Using sticks and kindling I found in the garage, I had a fire crackling in the small black kettle a few minutes later. Sitting on the patio, rubbing my hands with smoke drifting around my head, I felt like I was camping in the wilderness with God guiding me down unmarked trails.

After the embers faded, I trudged out into the deep snow to make twenty-eight snow angels, one for every year of our marriage. I lowered myself into the deep snow, spread my arms and legs, and stared at the clear sky sprinkled with stars above me. My breath formed puffs in the stillness. I picked up a handful of fresh snow and pushed the crystals into my mouth. I felt like Rose floating on a board after the

Titanic sank, clinging to Jack's dead body as it floated in the ice-cold water of the Atlantic. She loved Jack. Yet she knew when it was time to let him go. Six months had passed since John's death. I had hung onto him long enough. It was time to let go and move on. I managed to make eighteen snow angels before my numb cheeks and tingly hands drove me into the house.

Drained from the skiing and my snow angel project, I poured a glass of sherry and turned on the kitchen television. I flipped through the channels and landed on *The History of Rock and Roll* on our local public television station. The voices of Elvis, the Everly Brothers and Ricky Nelson curled through my head and triggered memories of my years as a teenager. I remembered dancing around the living room floor in my socks as the Everly Brothers sang "Wake Up Little Susie." I dreamed of falling in love, getting married and having lots of children.

That night when Ricky Nelson's face flashed across the television screen, my heart fluttered. Ricky, my dreamy-eyed teenage idol, strummed his guitar and sang "Lonesome Town." The song lyrics filtered through the screen. Alone on New Year's Eve I stared at the television. I felt like I was in my own town of loneliness with my broken heart and shattered dreams. I wondered if canceling out of New Year's Eve dinner with friends had been a mistake. Maybe spending time with the group would have filled the empty space and pushed away my sadness. Before Dick Clark rang in 2001, I was in bed.

With 2000, the worst year of my life, behind me, I committed myself to making it on my own. I knew 2001 would be better. All the books I read said the first year was the worst. I thought, "Get through the first year and I'll be fine." Over the next several months I spent time in local bookstores, studying the shelves of grief books I had not read yet. I hoped to find the answers I really needed to "move on." I checked the local paper for information on grief groups in the area. Finally, after calling several numbers on my list, I decided to join one. I thought it might help.

A week later after a long day at work, I bundled up in my winter clothes, crawled into my frigid car and drove to Trinity Lutheran Church in Stillwater. Under the glow of the parking lot lights, I locked the car behind me. Shuffling my boots along the snow-covered asphalt, I focused my eyes on the arch-shaped church entrance. I wrapped my glove around the heavy iron door handle and pulled it open. A flow of warm air wrapped around me. I wound my way through the empty corridors of the church, past a green banner with a gold cross and down the steps to the church basement. In a small room, gathered around a table, three gray-haired women sat across from a man. I unwrapped the wool scarf from my neck and settled into the cold folding chair.

The man welcomed us to the group and introduced himself as a pastor at the church. Then he asked us to share something about our loss and why we came to the group. I shifted my weight on the chair. Listening to the stories of the women seated around the table, thoughts tumbled through my head. Most of the women were in their mid to late eighties, had been married for almost fifty years, had adult children and several grandchildren. When my turn came my heart raced in my chest. Pushing the tears back, I told them that my husband was fifty-four when he died, we never had children and now I was alone.

After an hour of talking about death and the stages of grief, the pastor ended the session with a prayer and we said our goodbyes. Walking through the dark parking lot I thought, how lucky those women were to have so many years to share with their husbands. I felt cheated—not enough time, retirement dreams unfulfilled, and no grandchildren. Driving down County Road 18 with my Indian flute tape playing, I thought about the session. The pastor didn't tell us how to get through our losses. His vague phrases "lean into the grief . . . healing takes time . . . be kind to yourself" brought little comfort and did not magically heal my pain.

CHAPTER **13**

I Can Do It!

WITH CHRISTMAS BREAK over and the holidays behind me, I returned to work with an "I can do it!" attitude. I focused on planning lessons for classrooms, leadership team meetings and preparing for staff training sessions. In spite of my positive attitude, my days continued to be a physical and emotional stretch. My heart constantly raced. Aches consumed my body. I felt like I could die. The stress at work coupled with my nightly loneliness was unbearable. Overwhelmed and exhausted from trying to accept the changes in my personal life and from trying to motivate the staff to make major changes in their teaching life, my weekly prayer was, "God, get me to Friday."

On the days I could hold my grief at a distance, visiting classrooms energized me. Animated kindergartners wrapped their arms around my waist when I walked into their Writer's Workshop. Sitting next to them on their miniature chairs or on the floor by the alphabet chart, they snuggled next to me. With pride they read their stories written in squiggles and giant capital letters. When I struggled to get out of bed in the mornings, the students' faces pulled me up and helped me put my feet on the floor. The combination of the students' energy and the unconditional support from Jane and Linda made my days bearable and helped me take small steps forward in my life.

Shortly after winter break, we were back on an airplane, flying to a national conference in Jacksonville, Florida. As the airplane hummed through the sky, I sipped a glass of white wine and reviewed my notes for our presentation. I wondered how could our team possibly explain to an audience of administrators, teachers and literacy experts how to successfully implement a school-wide literacy improvement program when we had only been working on it for four months. I wondered, *Whose crazy idea was it to do this presentation anyway?*

When we arrived at the hotel we discovered it was in the process of a major renovation. I was disappointed that the pool was closed for construction. My colleagues were more concerned about the unfinished conference room where we would be presenting. The night before our presentation, and after a few cocktails, our team decided to check the renovation progress on the conference room and practice our presentation. When the elevator doors bounced open, we walked into a hallway covered with strings of wires and scraps of carpeting. Stepping over the construction debris, we located our room. We tried to flip on the lights, but the power must have been off. We ended up sitting in the hallway. We talked through the presentation and tried to figure out a back-up plan in case there was no projector or video access.

By the time we walked back to our rooms my nerves were frazzled. The antidepressant the doctor prescribed a month earlier had not provided much relief from the pain, but I continued to take the tiny white pills, praying for better days ahead. With the stressful presentation looming over my head, sleep escaped me as I tossed and turned in bed. The next morning I waited for the phone to ring with hopes that someone would tell me our presentation was canceled. No luck. As they say in show business, the show must go on—and we did.

Luckily the room was finished and the lights worked. Other than the unexpected fire alarm that evacuated the conference rooms for several minutes, our presentation came to a successful end. The audience enjoyed our "Patience" video. Relieved to have the presentation over, we spent the balance of the week attending sessions, meeting new friends and enjoying Jacksonville's warm weather and sunshine.

Our trips became a respite from the daily stress of our jobs. I started to actually look forward to packing my suitcase and flying away to a distant destination.

After returning from sunny Florida, within weeks Linda, Jane and I were back on an airplane headed for Herndon, Virginia, three miles from the Dulles International Airport. Our hotel, like many we stayed in for trainings, was located in an area with not even a shopping mall in walking distance. After our daily sessions filled with hours of sitting and eating, instead of venturing out for a long walk we quickly returned to our rooms. Within minutes after dropping off our binders, we reconvened in the lobby bar for cocktails. As we sipped martinis and wine, a piano player dressed in a suit floated his fingers across the ivory keys of a black baby grand piano. After a glass of wine, I walked over to the piano player. He asked if I had a song request. Without thinking I asked him to play the theme song from *A Man and a Woman*. The 1966 French movie tells the story of a widow and widower who fall in love when their paths cross. I asked him to play it in memory of my husband. The man smiled and motioned for me to join him on the cushioned bench. The song, one of John's favorite pieces to play on the piano, triggered memories of our life together.

When he finished the song, I thanked him and got up to join my friends. He stood up, closed the cover on the piano keys, and asked if I would like to join him for a drink during his break. Maybe it was the wine talking, but I accepted the invitation and followed him into the dark cocktail lounge. We slid into chairs at a table for two, and he asked what I would like. I said a brandy and water would be fine. He ordered a scotch on ice for himself, a triple. As we sipped our drinks he puffed on a cigarette. He told me he had performed at national concerts, but now he worked part time for the Hilton Corporation. He had been married twice, was divorced and lived in Mexico by the ocean.

After we finished our drinks, he said he had to go back for his next set. He snubbed out his cigarette in the glass ashtray in the center of the table, and we headed for the lobby. I was impressed that he could find the right keys after several shots of scotch. Before he finished the set, I told him I had to leave. My friends were waiting for me upstairs. He said his last day at the Hilton was Friday, then he was headed back to Mexico.

Riding up in the elevator, my head swirled. I wondered what went wrong with his two marriages. He was the first man I had shared a drink with since John had died. He seemed nice enough. I realized I enjoyed his attention and our conversation over drinks. I had no plans of jumping in bed with him or catching the next plane to Mexico, but I hoped I would see him again. When I walked into the room my colleagues bombarded me with questions. They wanted all the details. Trying to hide my flushed cheeks and avoid their questions, I poured myself a drink and focused on the *Friends* episode on the television.

Morning came too early. Thankful it was the last day of training I managed to shower and slam down two aspirin. I made it to the training session just in time to pour a cup of coffee and settle in before the trainer turned on her microphone. After the session, I looked for the piano man in the lobby, but he was not there. I headed to the pool. Floating on my back, I stared up at my reflection in the glass above. The cold water rolled over me and blended with my tears. I knew John would be proud of me for making it through the week. I heard his voice whisper, "I love you, Diane."

To save the school district money, Linda had booked a Sunday-to-Sunday flight. On Saturday a few of us headed for Washington, D.C., to do some sightseeing. Feeling trapped in the back seat of the rental car, I stared out the window at the gray skies. The first place we stopped was the Holocaust Museum. I wanted to join my friends on the tour, but knew the intense exhibit would be difficult for me to get through. I needed to walk in the fresh air and suggested they go ahead without me. At the last minute a literacy coach from another school who was pregnant decided to join me. We strolled along the National Mall, stopping at a few art museums along the way. After wandering through several exhibits, we found an empty bench on the mall by a skating rink where skaters twirled and glided along the ice.

As love songs poured out of the loudspeaker, I pictured John's warm smile and the sway of our bodies as we skated around the local rink on our first date in 1971. Without John, my life was broken, and I had no idea how to fix it.

Rereading the scribbled entries in my journal on the flight back to Minneapolis, I realized my life was a mess. I had to accept the fact that John was never coming back. I thought, "Change the way you think and start exercising. Stop worrying about the future. Live in the present. Hang on to the memories. They'll always be there." I bought another glass of chardonnay to celebrate my new plan.

My plan lasted three days. On Valentine's Day I forced myself out of bed. Staying in bed was not an option. My principal who had given me the lead to my literacy coach position was coming to our school for a visit. I couldn't let her down. When I arrived at school, students greeted me with hugs and candy hearts that said, "I Love You." Paper hearts and Valentine bags dangled in every classroom I visited. Memories of red roses, romantic cards and our Valentine's Day dinner at the Rainbow room in New York crashed through my mind. Living in the present was harder than I thought.

When my principal arrived we gave each other a long hug. I pushed back my tears. She admired the student writing and standards on the hallway bulletin boards. As she observed in the second grade Writer's Workshops, she was amazed that they were reading nonfiction books, writing reports about sea animals and typing their stories on the computer. Before she left, she smiled and hugged me again.

Valentine's Day sucked. I wanted to cuddle up with John and fall asleep in his arms. Instead, I called the piano player. No answer. I left a message with my phone number and told him how much I enjoyed listening to his music. Before I hung up, I wished him a Happy Valentine's Day. I sat next to John's eight-by-ten photo, the one I took on every training trip. I wondered if the piano player had a yacht, if he ran on the beach or if he loved the ocean as much as I did. I pictured him serenading me on a balcony in the Mexican moonlight. I even thought I might take guitar lessons again or learn how to play John's piano. For several days I waited for a call from the piano player. It never came.

By March I was ready for the endless Minnesota winter to be over. The winter days gained a few minutes of daylight each day and gave me hope for brighter days ahead. Robins returned, first a few and then in flocks. With the uplifting signs of spring, my mood improved. I started walking and exercising. I still felt anxious at times, but figured it was just job stress. Feeling better, I weaned myself off of the anti-depressant and focused on summer vacation in June. In mid-March, Jane, Linda and I flew back to Jacksonville for the last training of the year. This time, without a presentation looming over our heads, we could focus on the sessions and enjoy Jacksonville's eighty-degree weather. I looked forward to my first year of grief coming to an end in June, believing the next year would be easier.

I spent Easter with my sister and her family. In May I attended my nephew's wedding in Duluth, Minnesota, a quaint city perched on the edge of Lake Superior. The morning of the wedding, I drove the three-hour drive north alone. Sporadic tears dripped off my chin as the familiar scenery zoomed by. I thought of all the times I had driven alone to northern Minnesota when my mother was dying. Memories of childhood trips to my grandparents' farm and Lake Superior vacations with John careened off the birch and pine trees nestled along the highway. I forced myself to focus on the traffic and the endless highway ahead.

After checking into a local motel on the outskirts of Duluth, I unpacked my overnight bag, hung my dress in the closet and started a pot of coffee. Staring into the bathroom mirror, my hand trembled as I rolled the blue eyeliner along my lower lid and stroked blush across my cheeks. I pulled on my dress, combed my hair and headed for the car. I nestled the Probe into a parking place not far from the church entrance. I was relieved to see Mike and Mary and her family standing in the entryway, waiting for me. We sat together in a pew and stood up as the radiant bride walked down the aisle. I scanned the crowd, but John and my brother Tom were nowhere.

Dizzy and weak, I blotted tears away with the crumbled hanky tucked in my hand.

After the ceremony, I followed Mary and Al to the reception at a resort overlooking Lake Superior. Couples laughed, danced and raised their glasses in a toast to the newlyweds. Sitting alone at the table, I sipped my wine and watched Mary and Al dance. After a few polkas with my brother, I said my goodbyes to the bride and groom. Alone, I walked out into the crisp northern Minnesota spring air. The sound of my footsteps echoed on the gravel parking lot and a shiver rolled across my shoulders as I eased the Probe onto the dark highway. Sitting on the bed in my hotel room, I sobbed. I told John and my brother Tom how beautiful the wedding was and how much I missed them both.

During the long drive home, memories of my childhood floated through my head. I saw images of my parents and my brother sitting at the breakfast nook at our tiny house in North Minneapolis. I heard Kate Smith's voice on the radio singing "When the Moon Comes Over the Mountain." Images of *The Howdy Doody Show* on our black-and white-television flashed through my mind. I remembered crying when Buffalo Bob said "Goodbye" the day the show went off the air. Difficult as it was to leave the past behind, with John gone, moving forward was my only option. The memories would move with me.

CHAPTER **14**

Comfort

THINKING MY JOURNEY through grief would be like a fifty-yard dash and my life would return to normal when I crossed the one-year finish line in June, I kept pushing ahead. However, no matter how hard I tried, I still struggled to get through my days. My brother Tom's and John's deaths had created an intense anxiety about my own mortality. Life continued to be a daily process of putting one foot in front of the other and just getting through it. Tired and exhausted, my life tilted and swayed while my heart slammed in my chest. I felt like I was dying. Every afternoon the dismissal bell signaled the end of the day. When the children filed by my office with their packs bobbing on their backs and smiles stretched across their faces I knew I had made it through another day.

One gray spring afternoon as I drove home, a sharp pain ran across my chest. I gripped the steering wheel, praying the ache would stop. When the pain intensified I panicked. Instead of heading home on Interstate 94, I took the I-494 exit and drove to the hospital where my clinic was located. Terrified I was having a heart attack, I pulled into the emergency room parking lot. I sat in the car and tried to calm myself down, but nothing helped. My breathing quickened. My heart raced. Afraid I was dying, I ran toward the ER doors. Part of me wanted to turn back, but something pushed me on.

I told the nurse at the desk I thought I was having a heart attack.

She guided me into a curtained area where she checked my pulse and blood pressure. A doctor appeared carrying a chart and a clipboard in his hand. He jotted down my symptoms and directed the nurse to run a few tests. After an EKG and a blood draw, the nurse hooked up an IV and rolled me into a private room. She adjusted my blanket, nestled the call button next to me and said she would be back shortly with my dinner.

For the first time since the night of John's death, a sense of comfort rolled over me. When my supper arrived, I devoured the salad, vegetables and chicken. Even though the meal was served on a plastic tray, it tasted like a gourmet meal prepared at a fine restaurant, quite the change from microwave popcorn and frozen dinners. After dinner I called my sister to tell her I was in the hospital and left a message at work that I would not be there in the morning. Later, the nurse stopped in to check my monitors and helped me wheel my IV into the bathroom. She settled me back into bed and said my doctor would run tests in the morning. Then she handed me a small cup with a white pill in it and poured me a glass of water. She said the pill would help me sleep. I swallowed the tablet and leaned back into the newly fluffed pillows. Feeling drowsy, I clicked off the television and closed my eyes. The hum of voices in the hallway lulled me to sleep.

In the morning a nurse wheeled me into a dark room for an ultrasound. A young woman smeared the cold gel on my abdomen. She studied the screen as the sensor rolled along my skin. Respiratory tests and chest x-rays followed. Not sure what they were looking for, I just hoped they could make me better. Shortly after the nurse wheeled me back to my room, my sister arrived. She hugged me and then settled into a cushioned chair by the wall. I don't remember what we talked about—probably the gray weather and other everyday things. I told her about the tests and that the doctor planned to meet with me that afternoon or the next morning.

Before she left she hugged me again and told me to call her when I got the results of the tests. Alone in the room, I wondered if coming to the hospital was a mistake. I spent the afternoon flipping from one soap opera to the next. Every time a nurse passed by, my eyes darted toward the door, hoping my doctor would appear. By dinnertime, still no doctor. I called work again to tell them I would be out for a few more days. In the morning, my doctor arrived with a stethoscope dangling around his neck. When he pulled a chair up next to the bed, my heart raced in my chest.

"Well, Diane, everything looks normal. No heart problems, lungs are fine. Thyroid is in the normal range. What you experienced was a panic attack often triggered by stress or trauma. A small dose of an anxiety medication will help. There are also relaxation and breathing exercises that might help." He told me to pick up the prescription at the hospital pharmacy and asked me to call his office to schedule a follow up appointment.

When the doctor left, a nurse disconnected my IV, removed my clothes from the closet, and told me she would be back after I got dressed. Sitting on a cold chair in the room, my stomach churned. I buttoned my slacks and pulled my turtleneck over my head. Waiting for the nurse I stared at the comfortable hospital bed, wishing I could stay. The nurse rolled a wheelchair into the room, but I waved it away, assuring her I was fine. She escorted me to the front lobby and wished me well. After stopping at the pharmacy, I walked out into the parking lot.

Relieved to see the Probe in the parking lot right where I left it, I hit "unlock" on the key fob. I clicked my seatbelt in place and headed home. The garage door slammed shut behind me, and my footsteps echoed on the ceramic kitchen floor. The empty house said, "Welcome home." Nothing had changed. The next day I returned to work to "welcome backs" and "we missed you." In the hallway a kindergarten student wrapped his arms around my waist, smiled and said, "Ms. Hohl you are a **GOOD** teacher." The hugs and warm welcome backs made me feel better.

On top of my emotional dives, the daily job stress and challenges of home ownership continued to test my commitment to hanging on to the house. The second mortgage we took out to complete the remodel loomed over my head. With only my teaching salary, the monthly mortgage, taxes and bills consumed a large chunk of my check, leaving a small reserve for servicing water softeners, broken home appliances and repairing lawn equipment. When school ended in June, so did my paychecks until September. I wanted to make it on my own without touching the limited life insurance money in the bank. I considered selling the house again, but my attorney's advice kept echoing in my mind, "Don't make any major decisions for at least a year."

I welcomed summer vacation, believing my year of grief would soon end, my delusional thinking would disappear and my life would be back to normal. However, a major summer storm proved me wrong. The inch of water covering the laundry room floor was not a new problem, just one we had never solved. John and I had been told the problem was due to the slope of the patio. Determined to find a permanent solution, I called a cement company. The young guy surveyed the patio from several angles and decided tearing out the concrete and installing a new patio with a different slope would solve the problem. He assured me the project would only take a day and he could repair the two cracked sections of the driveway at the same time.

A couple of weeks later on a Friday morning his crew arrived with a dumpster and their equipment. Watching the crew of muscular guys saunter down the driveway, I stared at their tan bodies decorated with tattoos and body piercings. All of them had tightly clipped haircuts except the dark-haired guy with sideburns and a gold bracelet draped along his wrist. The crew looked nothing like the twenty-year-olds I knew back in the 1970s. These guys were young enough to be my kids. Soon, all I could hear was the sound of jackhammers drilling into the concrete. After an hour, the noise suddenly stopped.

The crew leader sauntered toward me and said the concrete was much deeper than he had anticipated. He needed a skid steer to pull up the slab and assured me he could have one on sight within an hour. Considering they had already torn out the shrubs surrounding the patio and a section of concrete, there was no turning back. The dark-haired guy continued to pick away at the patio with his jack-hammer, while his buddy pitched pieces of concrete into the dump-ster. By the time the skid steer arrived, the thermometer on the garage registered just shy of ninety degrees. During their smoke break, the guys peeled off their T-shirts and wrapped them around their heads to soak up the sweat. I stared at the dark-haired guy's tattoo, a red and black zigzag shaped lightning strike that ran down his back and ended in an arrowhead just above his tight jeans. The skid steer at-tacked the concrete, pulling up huge chunks of cement entangled in heavy-duty rebar.

Trying to escape the heavy equipment's constant drone and the clumps of concrete careening into the dumpster, I sought refuge in the house and retreated to the lower level. The artwork hanging on the walls rattled and pieces of plaster fell off the bar ceiling as the skid steer pounded on the patio outside. Shaking, I stood in the bar and covered my ears. Questioning my patio replacement decision, I screamed, praying the noise would stop. With the sun nestled on the edge of the horizon, the machinery finally fell silent. The crew leader explained that he never thought the project would take this long, but promised they would be back first thing in the morning before the cement truck arrived.

In the morning before I poured my first cup of coffee, the crew appeared in the driveway refreshed and ready for another day. The young guy in charge apologized again for the delay and offered to throw in a sidewalk to the front door for no charge. A small compen-sation for all the stress, but I accepted the offer. Before the cement truck arrived, the crew dumped wheelbarrows of sand into the patio space, leveled the surface and installed the rebar while the young guy sketched a rough diagram of the sidewalk design.

The clear sky provided no relief from the relentless sun's scorch-ing heat. By the time the cement truck roared down the road and backed into the driveway, the thermometer read ninety-five degrees. Two young guys, dressed in jeans and rubber boots encrusted in dry cement, steadied the blue cement chute while the others sloshed around, spreading the wet mixture over the rebar. The afternoon heat became their worst enemy. They worked quickly trying to get the surface smooth before the cement hardened. Writing the check for a few thousand dollars was painful, but solving the water problem was worth it.

Summer break stressed my cash flow, but renewed my energy. I bought relaxation tapes and scheduled regular massage sessions with my therapist. On John's birthday in June, two days before the first anniversary of his death, I drove to the cemetery with a bouquet of flowers I picked from the memorial garden I had made in our yard. I sat on top of his grave, soaking in his spirit. The *clang, clang* of a wind chime in the distance reminded me of the Big Sur cypress trees and fog. I felt all our love wrapped up in the gift of memories. With my finger I traced his name on the granite gravestone. I stared at the "Together Forever" that connected our names. Before leaving, I kissed John's gravestone and promised him I'd keep going no matter what happened.

Before school started in the fall, I spent the last several weeks eating better and exercising, trying to lose the additional pounds I had gained eating all the meals on training trips and dining out with friends. Every day I spent an hour on the bike path either walking or in-line skating to tunes on the oldies channel. After dark I drove to the grocery store. Without carts packed in the aisles, I lingered among the produce. After checking the items off my list, I dodged the snack aisles and headed for the empty checkout lane. Friends complimented me on my trim body and renewed spirit.

In late August, I met with my financial advisor. I decided to finally invest John's life insurance money in the stock market. My advisor assured me I was making the right choice. Within a few minutes he rolled the money out of my savings account and into an investment portfolio. I signed a few forms, shook his hand and walked out into the bright afternoon sunshine. Thinking of the widows I had met who were left with limited incomes, debts and bankrupt business investments, I considered myself lucky. I knew the money could never make up for the loss of John, but I felt more secure knowing it was there. By the time I returned to work with the first year of grief behind me, I felt healthier, a few pounds lighter, and emotionally stronger.

Returning to work in August, after a summer of house repairs, I looked forward to my first paycheck. A sense of relief rolled over me when the secretary handed me my check at the end of the first week. I ripped the envelope open and immediately filled out the authorization form to spread my pay over twelve months. I knew the monthly amount would be less, but the assurance of a check arriving in the mailbox twice a month in the summer brought me peace of mind. To supplement my teaching salary I decided to teach a class at the University of Wisconsin–River Falls, a thirty-mile drive from my school. The first Tuesday session at River Falls was also my first day with students at school, one of the most stressful days of the year. I spent most of Labor Day weekend organizing materials and writing out detailed plans for the three-hour session at the university. On Monday night I loaded everything in the car so I would be ready to leave early for work in the morning. That night I sat on the dark patio alone and toasted the start of a new school year and my literacy instructor position at the university. With the hardest year of grief behind me, I knew the months ahead would be better.

The first day of school was busy as always. Excited students dressed in their new school clothes stepped off the buses. They smiled at me as I marked their hand with a blue marker, a reminder of which bus to look for when they left in the afternoon. Once we got all the students to their new classrooms, I returned to our office. I missed my teammate Jane who had taken a literacy coach position in another school. With her gone, I tried not to worry about all the additional responsibilities ahead. Meetings with the principal and visits to classrooms kept me moving all day. When the last kindergarten student disappeared through the door, I headed for the car. With the click of my seatbelt, I pulled out of the parking lot and drove east on I-94.

With students arriving at 5:00, I barely had time to arrange the room and organize my materials. When the thirty students settled into the room, all I saw was a sea of exhausted faces. Knowing many of them had survived their stressful first day, I kept the session low key and upbeat. We introduced ourselves and reviewed the syllabus. I gave them time to go to the university bookstore to purchase the books for class. A few minutes before 8:00 p.m. they packed up their books and headed out the door. I pulled my suitcase through the dark, empty parking lot and loaded everything into the trunk. The evening tumbled through my head as I drove south on Highway 35. Images of the students' attentive faces signaled a positive start to the semester.

ﾉﾉﾉﾉﾚ

A week later on Tuesday morning the alarm buzzed me out of a deep sleep. I shuffled to the bathroom, flushed the toilet and clicked on the television. Images of the World Trade Center spewing flames and smoke out of the top floors flashed across the screen. Thinking it was an advertisement for a movie, I froze in front of the television and stared at the flaming image. A man's voice shouted, "Two Boeing 767 jets have crashed into the World Trade Center! People on the lower floors are streaming out. The top floors are buried in fire and smoke."

Glued to the screen, I stepped into my slacks, slipped my arms into a blouse and headed for the kitchen. I grabbed my lunch from the refrigerator, poured coffee into a traveling mug and loaded my materials for class into the car. I turned on the radio. A voice yelled, "Thick smoke is preventing any airborne evacuation. People on the top floors of the north tower are jumping to the ground!"

When I arrived at school, the flaming towers flashed across the television monitor in our office. Linda and I sat in silence, surrounded with the sounds of destruction and death. A somber mood hung in the classrooms and fear filled the faces of teachers as they passed each other in the hallways throughout the day. Before leaving for my class at River Falls, I called another instructor at the university to see if they canceled evening classes. As far as she knew, no classes had been canceled. During class that evening, the conversation focused on the terrorist attacks and how their schools tried to deal with the shock and devastation. I dismissed class early, knowing the students were exhausted and anxious to go home to their families. After the long, lonely drive home, I dumped my suitcase of teaching materials in the study, poured myself a brandy and turned on the television.

Words of war and photos of the collapsed towers flowed across the screen, rubble everywhere, and thousands of people dead. *How could this be happening in the United States, the most powerful and secure country in the world?* I thought the earth was coming to an end. I wanted to hold John and bury my face in his shirt. I clutched John's picture and wept for all the innocent people who died in the attacks and their families who would never hug them again.

CHAPTER

Grief Marathon

TWO WEEKS AFTER the horrific 9/11terrorist attacks, Linda and I were headed for a training session in Cincinnati, Ohio. Armed military guards patrolled the hallways of the Minneapolis–Saint Paul International Airport. The gray plastic tubs filled with our shoes, jackets and miscellaneous parts of our lives rumbled along the conveyor belt as we walked through the metal detector, looking straight ahead. Grim faces filled the chairs and gift shops along the concourse. With two hours before our flight, we joined colleagues from another school for breakfast.

All the relaxation and calm I had stored up from summer vacation had disappeared within the first few days of the new school year. My stomach whirled around as I stared at the Chili's menu. Nothing appealed to me, but I settled on a breakfast taco. Plastic spoons and forks had replaced the metal eating utensils, and there were no knives anywhere. Picking at the tortilla shell with my plastic fork I realized how the terrorists had changed every part of our lives. The thought of a Bloody Mary or screwdriver passed through my mind, but I hoped the early morning pill would squelch the anxiety storm brewing inside of me.

Gray skies and a hotel in the middle of nowhere greeted us in Cincinnati. During the continental breakfast before the first session, I spied Jane and waved to her. We wound our way through the crowd and hugged. She tipped her head to the side, looked me in the eye and asked how I was doing. "Great," I answered, which was a lie. The session started with a memoir study with the trainer reading children's books to us about death and loss. Not my favorite topic. I looked forward to the morning break, hoping a tray of chocolate chip cookies would be waiting for me.

The first night alone in my room, I stared out the window at the full moon's glimmer on the Ohio River. I thought of all the sunrises and sunsets John and I had enjoyed together. The warmth of his arms wrapped around me. My life felt more settled now than a year ago, but the loss still followed me everywhere. Nothing magical had happened at the end of the first year of grief. John was still gone. Instead of a 50-yard dash, my journey through grief seemed more like a grueling marathon that required endurance and strength to reach the finish line.

Every day after the endless sessions, a group of us headed for the local saloon across the parking lot from the hotel. We propped our feet up on the rickety deck in the sun and sipped oversized glasses of wine as we "debriefed" our day. The saloon reminded me of a rustic northern Minnesota bar. Beer banners hung in a line above the "SALOON" sign painted on the back wall. Next to the sign was a painting of a pig and a man with a sign on his back: "Bancroft Provision Dealers—Beef, Tripe, Sausage." The pool table light hung at a slant above the worn pool table where young guys lined up their cue shots, surrounded by a cloud of smoke.

A man at the bar stared at me. "Too young," I thought. But hoping he would ask me to dance, I picked up my wine glass with my left hand to display my bare ring finger. Instead, he grabbed a young blonde and whirled her out onto the dance floor. Flashbacks of The Honey Bee, a bar my college friend and I ended up at on our trip to Chicago in the seventies. We were very naïve back then, but it didn't take us long to realize we were in a "pick up" bar. The "SALOON" gave me the same feeling, but I didn't care. I was fifty-four and loved to dance.

I ordered another glass of chardonnay and joined the group of line dancers. Standing in the front row next to a guy in an Abercrombie "21" Athletics shirt, I swung my hips and slid to the music. After another round of drinks the group coaxed me up to the karaoke mike. We sang Neil Diamond's "Forever in Blue Jeans," one of my favorite in-line skating tunes. Not sure if it was the drinks or men on my mind, every time the song's refrain appeared, I sang "reverend in blue jeans."

On the morning flight back to Minneapolis, I focused on the training manual spread open on my tray, but my mind wandered to my brother Tom's oldest son's wedding that afternoon in Forest Lake, forty minutes north of Afton. As always my empty house welcomed me home. After refreshing my makeup, I quickly changed into a tan top, black skirt and heels, dragged a brush through my hair and climbed into the car. With the MapQuest directions on the seat beside me, I found the church and arrived a few minutes before the service. Sitting next to my sister, I wished my brother Tom had been there to see his oldest son, standing at the front of the church next to his beautiful bride.

After the ceremony, golden October leaves and blue skies surrounded my Godson and his bride as they posed by Tom's classic Edsel. The newlywed's beamed as cameras clicked in the autumn air. At the reception, surrounded by my family, I sipped wine and smiled as my brother-in-law snapped photos. Dinner conversation, delicious food and more wine filled the empty space next to me.

When the dancing started, John's absence crashed through me. Locked in the bathroom, I pleaded with God to bring my lover back. To no avail. So I wiped my eyes, blew my nose and returned to the reception. After a few dances, I said "goodbye" to my family and headed home. Exhausted from a week of training and the wedding, I poured myself a nightcap and crawled into my sweats. In my notebook, I filled several pages with details about the beautiful wedding. I told John that my missing him was deep as his grave, and that my life, still broken, was on the mend.

In November the stress of driving to the university on Tuesdays to teach after a hectic day of meetings and observations began to wear on me. After teaching for three hours and navigating the Probe along the dark, icy roads I worried about sliding into the ditch and landing in a snowdrift. The only numbers I had in my cell phone were my sister's, my neighbor's and AAA's.

Driving home after class on December 5 sharp pains ran across my chest. Trying to focus on the road ahead of me, I took deep breaths to relax and tried visualization exercises like the anxiety book suggested. Nothing helped. I swung off I-94 in Hudson and headed for the hospital emergency room. I tried to turn the car around twice, but a force kept driving me forward. I parked the Probe under a light in the parking lot. Snowflakes collected on my coat as I trudged through the snow toward the emergency room door.

The doctor on duty took my vitals while the nurse scattered sticky electrode patches across my chest and on my arms for an EKG. Goosebumps covered my arms and a chill ran through my body. I closed my eyes, trying to relax. The nurse stood by my bed while the machine clicked and recorded my heart rhythms. The electrocardiogram came out normal. In spite of the results, the doctor decided to monitor me overnight. I called school and left a message that I would not be there in the morning. After a few more tests and breakfast, the doctor renewed my lorazepam prescription to control my anxiety attacks and sent me on my way.

Over the next few weeks, following the doctor's orders, I took the medication as directed. Feeling more relaxed during the last session of the university class, I invited the students to an after-Christmas get together at my house in February. We picked a date, and I told them I would e-mail them directions. At the end of class, they filled out their final evaluation sheets, and we wished each other a Merry Christmas. With class over and Christmas break just a week away, a sense of calm folded over me. I still had occasional bouts of dizziness, restless sleep and strange dreams, but figured those would disappear with the medication and relaxation during break.

With two weeks off, I enjoyed sitting up late, reading and sleeping late into the morning. One night in a deep sleep a voice called, "Diane, Diane." Thinking it was John I clicked on the light and searched the room, but only shadows filled the corners of our bedroom. Two-forty, the clock numbers glared at me. I clicked off the light, pulled the covers under my chin and squeezed my eyes shut. I was sure the voice was John's.

The next night as I sat alone at the dining room table, eating my microwave meal, something moved on the deck outside the sliding glass door. With only the Christmas lights draped along the deck railing for light, I stared, waiting for the shape to reappear. After several minutes I turned back to my cold green beans and chicken. I clicked the remote and my nightly *Friends* episode appeared on the screen. They were sitting around the kitchen table in Monica's apartment trying to convince Rachel to cut up her credit cards. Forcing her to become independent like they were.

During the commercial, I rinsed off my plastic tray. The black shape whirled by the sliding glass door again and curled back around revealing a white diamond on its chest. The *Friends* episode faded away as I walked over to the sliding glass door. *It' a black dog!* I then realized it was the dog barking that had woken me up. Not John's voice. The shape paced back and forth along the sliding glass door. As I bent down to get closer the dog bared its teeth at me. It certainly was not friendly. I tapped on the window and the black shape darted off the deck. Relieved it was not a coyote, I clicked off the television and headed for the lower level to read my *Self* magazine in front of the Christmas tree.

When I wandered into the kitchen in the morning, the dog was still on the deck. I walked over to the sliding glass door. The pile of black fur, curled in the corner of the deck, jumped up and disappeared into the woods. I pulled my winter coat over the top of my sweats, wiggled my boots on and headed out to get the morning paper. As I walked out the door, the winter air wrapped around my head and whisked my breath away. The wind burned my ears as my boots crunched along the snow-covered driveway. *Maybe the stray dog was a sign from God that I needed a pet for company.* I pulled out the Saturday paper curled in the plastic paper tube and trudged back to the house. The dog was back on the deck, but disappeared again as soon as I was within a few yards of the back door.

Feeling sorry for the dog, I dug a huge box out of the garage, positioned it in the corner of the deck and arranged an old blanket in the bottom. Not sure if it was a male or female I named it "Nick" in honor of Santa Claus. Later in the day, I drove into Hudson to Fleet Farm to buy a collar, leash and dog food. On the way back, I posted "Dog Found" notices on the local bulletin boards, hoping someone would call. Over the next couple of days the dog befriended me. We started taking walks and even played "fetch" together.

When my family came over for Christmas, Nick flashed an energetic smile and impressed them with *her* fetching skills. Sitting around the dining room table sipping wine after dinner, my family suggested I keep her. They thought she would be good company. After my family hugged me goodbye that night, I stared at the Christmas tree, contemplating Nick. In spite of our bonding and my family's suggestion, I hoped someone would call and claim the dog before I headed back to work after break.

After winter break, Nick was still with me. The January temperatures dropped below zero. I moved Nick's "house" into the garage. In the morning when I opened the garage door to go to work, Nick zoomed out and down the road, headed toward my neighbor's. I yelled, "Nick! Get back here!"

Focused on the neighbor's garbage can, Nick piled forward, tipping the container over. Knowing I couldn't catch her on foot, I backed the Probe out of the garage and sped up the driveway. By the time I drove the short distance to the neighbor's, Nick had torn the plastic garbage bag open and was sniffing through the contents. I slammed on the brakes, opened the passenger's door and screamed, "Nick! Get in here!" The dog looked up and jumped into the back seat with her tongue hanging out. Perched on the back seat, she beamed a smile at me. I returned her to the garage with a "bad dog" and headed for work.

On the drive home that afternoon, I realized that with my work and travel schedule, keeping Nick was out of the question. I checked the answering machine the minute I got home, hoping for a message from the owner. Nothing. I looked up numbers of local animal shelters; an ad for "The Ark" animal shelter caught my eye. It was the "world's largest 'no kill' animal shelter with a home like setting." The photo of a dog relaxing on a raised bed in front of a gas fireplace assured me this was the place for Nick. I dialed the number and explained my situation to the woman. She said she would send someone out that night to pick up the dog.

When the van pulled into the driveway, I worried that Nick would resist the animal control woman. Bundled in a jacket with heavy gloves in her hand, the woman asked where the dog was. I pointed to the garage. She opened the garage door just a crack and the dog's nose appeared. Nick stood calmly on the other side. The woman spoke softly to the dog and clipped the leash to her collar. Nick wagged her tail and bounced beside the woman. When she slid the van door open, Nick jumped right inside and snuggled up next to her teenage son, seated in the back seat. Nick looked right at home; so much for the loyalty of a dog. Watching the van pull out of the driveway, I knew I had made the right decision.

CHAPTER **16**

Night Invaders

CURLED IN THE corner of the blue sectional, wrapped in a wool blanket, I sipped the soothing brandy. The moonlight formed dark shadows on the snowdrifts piled outside the sliding glass door. I could not care less. January in Minnesota was almost as bad as death itself. Eighteen months had passed since my husband's funeral. The emptiness of life still overwhelmed me—my disconnected life, broken into minute pieces.

The bedraggled tree I had decorated for my second Christmas alone still stood in front of the window. I stared at the brown pine needles that covered the tree skirt, a result of lack of water and attention. Over the long months that followed the funeral, friends and relatives, tired of my dead husband stories and endless tears, faded away. The frenzy of phone calls and visits had disappeared. The supporters returned to their lives. I wanted to return to mine. The ice cubes tinkled as I lifted the glass to my lips and swallowed the last few drops of brandy. As I uncurled my legs to pour one more drink, a flash of fur zoomed across the carpet and disappeared behind the wooden console TV we bought in 1988. I screamed, "Damn, a mouse! Well, you can just stay there until morning. I can't deal with anything else tonight."

I unscrewed the brandy bottle, poured the brown liquid over the shriveled ice cubes in the bottom of my glass, and flicked off the light. As I trudged upstairs the Tom O'Neal "Morning Gladiolus" print hanging in the stairwell brought my mind back to an art gallery in Carmel, California. I stared at the photograph. I remembered standing with John in front of the framed photograph, marveling at its clarity and vibrant red blossoms perfectly arranged in the terracotta vase with the snake image molded on it. The gladiolus, surrounded by the heat of the southwestern afternoon sunlight, had pushed us to buy the print in spite of the fact that the swirled serpent, a sign of a bad omen, did not sit well with me.

I climbed the last three steps, flipped off the light and headed for bed. I tried to erase the memory from my mind, but John's smile and voice echoed through the lonely night noises that cracked and rattled in the dark corners of the lonely house. The crumbs of ice in the bottom of the glass bumped my lips as I tipped the last swallow of brandy into my mouth. The warm liquid calmed me as I gently slipped John's favorite shirt over my faded green sweats, crawled into our bed alone and wrapped the covers around me.

Sunday morning crept into our silent, empty bedroom. The frigid winter air crawled through the picture window in front of me, and a chill ran through my body one bone at a time. Struggling to keep John with me, I often inhaled the aroma of his cologne. The musky scent of John's cologne clung to the collar of his blue shirt wrapped around me and tricked my heart into thinking he would be at the dining room table reading his morning paper. I shuffled into the kitchen; his chair was empty and so was the coffee pot, another reminder. He was gone.

I reached for the drawer handle for a coffee filter, but the junk drawer rolled open instead. Paper clips were mixed in with the pencils, rubber bands were everywhere and several small black dots were scattered among the clutter and assorted keys. My eyes landed on a partially used book of matches from one of our California trips. The bent and torn cover gaped open and revealed a double row of match heads. I yanked open the utensil drawer and found more black spots in the corner of the spoon section. Frantically I opened cupboards and drawers. *Damn. Mice. I have mice in the kitchen.* The rodents had been everywhere. The rumpled matchbook called me back to the junk drawer. I stared at the matches, something was different, the red tips weren't quite right. They looked . . . chewed.

Oh my God, the mice had chewed the tips. They could have started a fire. The whole house could have burned down. I collapsed on the corner of the fireplace hearth, cradled my head in my hands and sobbed, "I give up. I can't go on alone. I hate this!" I screamed and paced around the kitchen yelling at God. Not the most appropriate behavior for a Sunday morning, but I didn't care. God obviously didn't care about me. My frustration and anger forced me back to bed. I woke up drained and confused, rolled over onto John's side of the bed and glanced at the clock radio: 11:00. I remembered the mouse mess in the kitchen. Relieved it was Sunday and I had not missed work, I crawled out of bed for the second time, slipped John's shirt off and hung it on the hook in the closet. Dressed in my faded green sweats, I headed for the kitchen. The thought of the mouse clean up overwhelmed me, but I had to deal with it before heading back to work on Monday.

Clicking on the minitelevision in the kitchen, a muscular guy appeared on the screen. His voice kept me company as he bragged about his miracle weight loss program. I unloaded all the utensils out of the drawers, jammed what I could into the dishwasher and soaked the rest in the suds-filled sink. I pulled on rubber gloves and scrubbed the empty drawer with a chlorine mixture to kill the germs. I moved on to the junk drawer, picked out the scissors, tape, garage keys and other assorted items I wanted to keep, then dumped the rubber bands, paper clips and expired coupons in the trash.

With the drawers finished, I emptied the lower cabinets one by one. Every fry pan, pot and whisk I touched reminded me of John and his love for cooking. With my rubber gloves submerged in the sudsy water, the health guy on TV dumped sliced bananas, strawberries and low-fat milk into a heavy-duty blender. He flipped the switch, spun the fruits and talked about how the healthy shakes had turned his life around. I doubted my frequent meals of microwave popcorn followed by several servings of ice cream spooned directly out of the cardboard carton were in his eating plan. Hoping to improve my eating habits, I grabbed the tablet by the phone, gripped the pencil with my rubber glove and scribbled the phone number as best as I could on the soggy tablet. I pulled off my gloves and dialed the number. A man's voice answered, "Hello, my name is Gerard. How can I help you today?"

"I want to order the blender I just saw on TV."

"I will be happy to send you the Ultimate Blender. If you order it today you get the free recipe book, a healthy food starter kit and for the next ten minutes we are offering a free exercise video that comes with it's own special exercise band."

What a great deal, I thought. The invisible voice typed as I recited my address, phone number and read off my credit card number. I pulled my wet rubber gloves back on, relieved that when the new blender arrived, my eating habits would miraculously improve and life would return to normal. As I placed each spatula, slatted spoon and knife into its new sterilized space in the drawer a voice started blabbing in my head, "You don't even cook and you hate grocery shopping. What were you thinking? The blender won't solve your problem. Don't waste your money. Cancel the order." I panicked; the voice was right.

I dialed the number and a new voice answered. I explained that the order had been a mistake and I needed to cancel it. After a conversation about the blender's benefits and the money-back guarantee, the voice canceled the order. With the utensils, pots and pans back in place, I sat down on the kitchen tile and peered into the corner lazy Susan cabinet. I wondered why I hadn't noticed the mouse signs before? Surveying the dark corner, I noticed a one-inch space between the cabinet wall and the counter top.

"Hmmm, I bet that's where they're coming up from the storage area." I found a box of steel wool and a metal mousetrap in the storage area and marched back up to the kitchen. A friend had told me that mice don't chew through steel wool. Stuffing strips of the steel wool into the crevice, I hoped she was right. As a second line of defense, I set a metal mousetrap on the floor under the lazy Susan and twirled the shelves back into place. Then I smeared peanut butter on three more mousetraps and strategically positioned them in the crawl space in the lower level storage area. Confident I had the nasty rodents under control, I headed upstairs, popped a huge bag of microwave popcorn, my reward for a job well done.

With no sign of dead mice in the morning, I packed my lunch into my rolling suitcase and headed for work. During the weeks following winter break, Linda and I made plans for our trip to the National Conference in Anaheim, California. We spent time observing in classrooms and made notes of the successful literacy strategies teachers were implementing into their daily instruction. Without having to do a presentation this year, Linda and I looked forward to attending the conference and networking with all the people we had met at our training sessions.

The photo on my desk of John and I sitting on the deck at Nepenthe's Restaurant in Big Sur reminded me of all the trips we had taken to California during our twenty-eight years of marriage. Visions of California beaches, palm trees and the Pacific surged through my mind. My excitement of seeing the Pacific coast again was clouded by my fear of an emotional downfall. I told Linda that this would either be my best travel trip so far or my worst. Her nod told me she understood.

The morning of our flight, we inched our way through the long security lines at the Minneapolis–Saint Paul airport. While walking down the concourse, I spied a friend of ours from John's years with the Minneapolis Aquatennial. The man's face lit up as he worked his way through the crowd. He wrapped his arms around me. I immersed myself in the scent of his aftershave and the crackle of his leather jacket. He looked in my eyes and asked how I was doing. I told him I still missed John deeply. When he asked why I was at the airport, I told him I had a new job and was headed to Anaheim. He invited me to join him in the Elite lounge where we could visit, but I told him I had a flight to catch. He said he would call me when he returned from his business trip to Europe. He never did.

Sitting on the plane, the aroma of his cologne lingered in my hair. His warm hug clung to my shoulders. I wondered if I could continue to live without the warm touch and intimacy John and I shared. Yet I struggled with the thought of losing someone I loved a second time. With the flight attendant standing in the aisle holding an oxygen mask, I promised myself that I would never marry again. Paging through my magazine, I looked forward to the California blue skies, the roll of the Pacific and the crunch of sand between my toes.

Shortly after we arrived at the hotel in Anaheim, a small group of us decided to drive to Hollywood for some sightseeing. Knowing we would be in sessions for the rest of the conference, I decided to tag along. A few minutes away from the hotel, I wanted to get out of the rental car, go back to my room, pull on my swimsuit and float around the pool. The rock music on the car radio agitated me. Stuck in traffic on the way back, I was ready to jump out onto the freeway. Relieved to be back at the hotel, I passed on the group dinner and retreated to my room. Riding up in the elevator, my heart crashed against my chest.

Back in the room I stretched out on the bed, took deep breaths and visualized peaceful trees and gently flowing rivers. Nothing helped. Trying to be healthy, I ordered a salad from room service. I told myself tomorrow would be better, and I retired early. Waves of anxiety and disconnected dreams interrupted my sleep. At 5:30 a.m. I crawled out of bed and wrote in my notebook about the empty hotel room and pointless dinners with wives complaining about husband's snoring or flipping channels. Sitting alone in the California hotel, I missed my husband's snoring and wished we were curled up together in the king-sized bed.

After our sessions were over, several of us drove to the ocean. Walking along the beach, I smelled the kelp and watched the sunset ripple along the waves. When I returned to the hotel, I just wanted to quit, to die and have it be over. I sat on the bed and cried so many tears that the Pacific Ocean seemed shallow. Being in Anaheim was a constant reminder of the loss. California overwhelmed me with emptiness.

The trip with its days that fell into nights turned into a nightmare filled with disjointed dreams and painful confusion. During the flight home I checked my watch every few minutes and counted the hours left before we landed at the Minneapolis–Saint Paul airport. Relieved to feel the jet's wheels rolling along the tarmac, I pulled my carry-on bag out from under the seat. When I heard the cabin attendant open the door, I slid into the moving line of passengers ahead of me. Linda and I said our goodbyes at the baggage claim area, knowing that fifteen hours later we would be back at work.

On Monday morning Linda and I met with our principal to review our conference session notes. We identified areas in reading instruction that our school needed to take deeper and discussed how we could provide more training time for the staff. After the meeting Linda and I returned to our office to plan for a reading literacy training session in New Jersey. Exhausted from the California trip and overwhelmed with the thought of another week of training just two weeks away, I felt nauseous and shaky. Thinking I was hungry, I choked down my microwave pizza lunch and an apple. By midafternoon I told my principal that I was not feeling well and needed to go home. I assured him I would be fine and planned to be back in the morning. I kept trying to prove to everyone, including myself, that I was making it on my own. It was a lie.

CHAPTER **17**

Amazing Grace

DISTRAUGHT AND ALONE, I gripped the steering wheel and drove as fast as I could. Pacing back and forth in the kitchen, I tried to squelch the pain. I found solace in my bed under layers of blankets. Picturing my life torn apart and no way to fix it, I couldn't face another day. When I woke up, darkness filled the bedroom windows facing the valley. I knew I was in trouble. A chill trembled through my body. Sitting at the dining room table I sipped a small bowl of chicken noodle soup while my television "Friends" kept me company. Planning to go to work in the morning, I laid my clothes out on the blue swivel chair in the bedroom and set my tennis shoes next to the bed with plans to exercise in the morning.

Trying to relax before bed, I sipped some tea and tried to read a magazine, but my agitated mind kept bolting from one image to the next. As a last resort, I poured a small glass of port wine and wound down the steps to the lower level to watch television. Shortly after midnight, I headed upstairs and crawled into the cold bed. Shivering, I pulled the covers up to my chin and squeezed my eyes closed, hoping sleep would bury the anxiety raging through my body.

A few hours later, the alarm clock jolted me out of an agitated sleep. I hit the snooze alarm and rolled over. When the alarm buzzed again, I shut it off. Exhausted, I stared out the window at the pastel sunrise. *Get up, Diane. Get downstairs and exercise.* My body refused to move. Hoping a cup of coffee would help, I crawled out of bed and shuffled down the hallway to the kitchen. With a cup of coffee in my hand, I paced around the house, crying. Nauseated, I crawled back in bed. I cradled the phone in my hand, buried my head in the pillow and sobbed. Weak and broken from the continuous, relentless months of grief and pain, my body craved a release.

After several attempts to get out of bed, I finally called work and told the secretary I was still not feeling well and was staying home to rest. She told me to take care of myself and hoped I felt better. Unable to quiet the anguish consuming my body, I paced around the living room holding the phone and I tried to convince myself I could make it through the loss alone. In spite of my positive "self-talk," anxiety and panic raged through my body. Terrified, I dialed 9-1 and hung up several times. Finally I pushed 9-1-1 and a static-filled voice answered, "911, what is the problem?"

"My husband died in June. I'm all alone and scared. I need help." My voice trembled as I gave the woman my name and address. After asking several other questions she said, "Diane, the paramedics are on their way. Can they get in?"

"No, the door's locked."

"Diane, go and unlock the door." She continued talking calmly to me while I walked to the front entry foyer and unlocked the door. I crawled back in bed. She kept me on the phone until two paramedics and the sheriff appeared in my bedroom.

"Diane?" I tilted my head up toward the voices.

"We're here to help you. Everything will be fine." I nodded.

"I'm just so sad. I want to get better." I clicked off the phone.

"Diane, do you have any medications in the house?" I shook my head forgetting about my anxiety medication in the bathroom. My mind covered in a fog tried to untangle the confusion flowing through the room. I could smell the cold clinging to the paramedics' jackets as their voices floated over my head. The familiar sound of the crackling radio conversations triggered flashbacks of the night I found John gone. As they talked to me, I remained frozen on the bed. Tears pooled in the corner of my eyes and dripped down my face. One paramedic walked out of the bedroom, while the other one stooped down next to the bed.

"Diane, are these your tennis shoes?" I nodded. "Can you put them on or do you want me to help you?" I rolled myself up and sat on the edge of the bed. The shoe felt heavy in my hand as I twisted my foot into it. My plan to exercise had seemed so logical the night before. I heard the rumble of the gurney cart roll across the ceramic tile foyer and into the hallway that led to the bedroom.

"Diane, do you want us to help you?" I shook my head. I wasn't sure why he wanted me to get on the cart. I just wanted someone to help make my life normal. Surrounded by the two paramedics and the county sheriff dressed in his tan uniform and leather jacket, I eased myself onto the cart. I stared up at the officer searching the bedroom with his gun strapped around his waist. He stopped in the doorway and asked, "Are there any guns in the house?"

I hesitated. "One." When he asked where it was I told him it was in the hallway closet, top shelf. The sheriff turned and marched out of the room. The closet door clicked open and glass vases clinked together as he rummaged through the shelves. My heart raced. *What had I done?* The woman paramedic pulled a blanket over me as they rolled the gurney down the hallway and into the foyer.

"Do you have a purse and a coat?" I pointed to the closet doors. The woman paramedic handed me my purse and spread my red coat over the cotton blanket covering me. When they propped open the front door, the exhaust from the paramedic van left running in the driveway nauseated me. The bitter cold January air clipped my cheeks as they rolled me out the door and lifted me into the van.

The paramedic van door slammed shut and a sudden sense of panic rose in my chest, my heart raced. *Where were they taking me?* I stared straight through the square window on the back door of the van. The image in the window resembled a photograph from the front page of a daily newspaper. There the sheriff stood in his leather jacket, holding my grandmother's Colt pistol in his hand. The gun, a family heirloom, had only been shot a few times by my brother Tom.

"He can't take that. It was my grandmother's gun. I need it back!"

The woman paramedic crouched next to me. "He wants you to know that he has the gun; you'll get it back. Don't worry."

"I shouldn't have called. I didn't know what to do. I'm so sorry." Behind my head, I heard the static-filled words of the paramedic's radio, "We have a woman who is depressed . . . husband died . . . alone." Over his shoulder he asked me, "Who's your doctor?"

"Harleson at Brookstone Hospital." The driver dispatched the hospital as he turned down the snow packed road. A message came over the radio, "No room at Brookstone. He said to take her to Hope Hospital in Saint Paul."

The woman paramedic stroked my arm. "You'll make it through this. You did the right thing calling us. You don't have to apologize. It's our job to help people."

"I just want to get better. I miss my husband so much." My body shook below the blanket.

"Are you cold, do you need another blanket?" I nodded, even though I was not sure if the chill was from the cold or the confinement of the van. The paramedic added one more blanket and tucked the sides around my body.

"I didn't want it this way, I want my life back the way it was."

"Diane, I can't imagine how hard it was to lose your husband. I was there the night he died. He was so young and handsome. I am so sorry you had to face his death alone. My dad was in your situation. He struggled for a long time, but now he's doing fine. You'll make it." The woman's compassion and understanding assured me that calling 911 was the right decision.

When we arrived at the hospital, the paramedics wheeled me through the emergency room door. Two nurses transferred me to another cart and pushed me down the hallway. The cold beige walls, fluorescent lights and the people's expressionless faces offered as much comfort as a bowl of bland oatmeal. They positioned the cart into a space and closed the curtain. The words depression and suicide filtered through the sheer fabric surrounding me. In spite of all the energy I spent painting on my smile every day, going to work and "moving on," that morning the hopelessness of living the rest of my life alone without John engulfed me and tumbled me into an invisible pit; one I knew I could not climb out of on my own.

In the frigid emergency room chills ran through me as the nurse continued her interrogation and wrote endless notes on her clipboard. "How old are you? Do you smoke? Drink alcohol? Any medications? Any family members die of cancer?"

I stared at my fingers. I wanted to go home. The nurse with the stethoscope dangling around her neck was abrupt and abrasive. She wanted too much information. I looked away as I heard the wheels of a patient's cart bump through the hallway beyond the gauze wall. My eyes stared at the heavy-set nurse as she jotted more notes on her paper without looking up.

"Emergency contact?" I hesitated, knowing my brother was at work and how far away my sister lived. I gave her Mary's name and phone number.

"Do you live alone?"

I nodded my head. The tears pushed against the back of my eyes as I swallowed. "My husband died eighteen months ago. He was all I had. I don't know what I'm going to do." The nurse handed me a tissue.

"Just try to relax. Let's get your blood pressure and pulse. I want you to slip off your clothes and put on this gown. It ties in the back. Can you take off your sweatshirt?" I nodded.

"I'll be back in a few minutes, so we can get your vitals and a urine sample." She slipped out of the room. The gray sweatshirt was my favorite. I wore it everywhere. A California cypress tree with the words *Pebble Beach* was imprinted on the left side above my heart, the broken heart I came to the hospital to get fixed. I crossed my arms and grabbed the bottom hem of the sweatshirt. The top plastic button caught my hair. After untangling my hair, I pulled my sweatshirt over my head. I slipped my arms into the short-sleeved gown and pulled the thin cotton blanket up to cover the goose bumps on my arms.

The nurse appeared from behind the curtain. She wrapped the blood pressure cuff around my thin arm and swirled her stethoscope off her neck. My heart throbbed in my chest as she pumped the rubber bulb in her hand and the cuff tightened. The idea of bolting from the room, filled with monitors, machines and cold hospital smell, flashed through my mind. I wanted to pull my sweatshirt on, grab my purse and leave the ER behind. The other part of me screamed, *No, Diane, stay. You need help. You can't go on like this.*

Sitting on the toilet, shivering with the thin gown draped over my scrawny body, I relaxed enough to finally dribble a urine sample into the plastic cup. The knock on the bathroom door startled me.

"Are you okay?" the nurse asked.

"Yeah." I washed my hands and walked out into the long, gray hospital hallway. I pulled back the gauze curtain screen where the nurse stood waiting for me.

"Sit down on the bed, and we will get you admitted." *Admitted? They planned on keeping me here?* I panicked. *Why can't they just give me medication and send me home? I can't stay.*

"We are very crowded right now, but have a bed available upstairs. When something else opens up, we'll move you." The nurse took me by the hand, helped me into a wheelchair and folded my red coat on my lap.

"We need to secure your valuables until we discharge you." I reached in my purse and handed her my wallet. She turned the wheelchair over to a young nurse who rolled me onto the elevator. The elevator hummed as it moved from floor to floor. The bell rang and the door slid open. The nurse rolled me down the hallway, past a nurse's station and up to a sliding glass door. She waited as a nurse behind a glass enclosure checked her records. A buzzer sounded and the door slid open.

Once inside, the door slid shut and the nurse wheeled me to a room with two beds. In the bed by the door, a woman faced the wall. The nurse gave me pajamas, booties and a blue robe to wear that identified me as a suicidal risk. She said the robe was for my protection, then helped me into the bed next to the window. After she hooked me up to the monitors and an IV that she would check through the night, she asked me when I ate last. When I told her I wasn't sure. She said she would bring me a breakfast tray. I spent the day staring out the window at the bare tree branches wiggling against the gray sky, wishing I had never made that morning phone call. *I didn't belong there.* I wanted to leave, but my clothes were locked up. The woman in the bed next to me coughed off and on, but never turned around or talked to me.

After my evening meal the nurse said she would be monitoring me for a couple days. Every hour she checked in on me. My roommate got up a few times to use the bathroom, then crawled back in bed and turned her face away. She held a small sheet of paper on the wall. I watched as her pen with a flower on the end wiggled across the paper.

When darkness settled over the room, I rolled over toward the window, wishing I would die. When the nurse checked on me she noticed I had been crying. A few minutes later she came back with a glass of water and a pill she said would help me sleep. I swallowed the tiny pill with a gulp of water. Tossing and turning, I tried to block out my roommate's snoring and coughing. Fading into a mellow euphoria, I eventually floated off into a dream about John. He smiled at me and looked healthy, strong and happy. When I woke up the next morning the dream lingered. Nothing made sense. I thought about John and heaven. The nurse walked in and unhooked the monitors. She told me that today I would be eating in the common area with the other patients. I told her I was tired and just wanted to sleep.

"The sooner you get up and participate in the group activities, the better. Believe me I was where you are right now and made it. You will, too. I expect to see you at breakfast in a few minutes." When the nurse left, the reality hit me that I was not in a hotel with room service, but in a secured ward. The nurses were monitoring me for severe depression. Crawling out of bed to join the other patients for breakfast took all the strength I had. I sat at a square wooden table with three other patients, two men and a woman. I picked at the food on my tray with my plastic utensils.

Thinking someone was probably watching me, I finished everything on my tray. Sitting at the table surrounded by strangers, I noticed all the patients were wearing blue booties. Some of them floated from place to place around the room, others just gazed out into the distance. Behind me a nurse explained to a man how to take his meds. Everyone's clothes and belongings were locked up. One young guy, upset about being there, paced the floor yelling, "Kick shit . . . I don't belong here!" The negative atmosphere and swearing agitated me. It was like living in an Eddy Murphy movie. *How did I get here?*

As soon as we cleared our trays, the nurse gathered us in the common area for a sing-along. Dressed in my pajamas and robe, I wedged myself in the corner of the couch. Another group of patients, dressed in their regular clothes, filed in the door and sat in a circle on the floor. A young man with a guitar smiled as he eased into a chair in front of us.

After tuning his guitar, he welcomed all of us and encouraged everyone to join him on his first song, "Amazing Grace." The lyrics triggered memories of John's funeral and the bagpiper standing in the parking lot. Tears dripped down my cheeks as I stumbled over words that told of lost souls that were finally saved. Our sing-along continued with camp songs like "Michael Row the Boat Ashore" and "This Land Is Your Land." The only thing missing was a campfire and marshmallows.

During our morning break, I sat alone on the couch as others wandered out to the enclosed patio for a smoke or made short calls from the community phone on a small table in the corner. When the fifteen minutes were over, a group leader led us down a stairway to what he called a "craft studio." The room looked like a workshop. He told us we could paint, color, or make a craft project. I thought about making a plastic sun catcher, but figured I would be going home soon, so decided to make a bracelet, something I could finish in one session. While I strung plastic beads on the vinyl string, "Amazing Grace" continued to roll through my head.

Having mastered the mealtime routine, at lunch I sat at the same table with two people I met at craft time. The young guy sitting across from me wanted to be a writer. We talked about writing. He told me he had taken classes at The Loft Literary Center in Minneapolis. I told him about my years of dabbling in writing, but that I had never taken classes at The Loft. He ripped a piece of paper off his tablet and scribbled the phone number and name of the Educational Director of The Loft, located on Washington Avenue in Minneapolis. When he handed it to me I thanked him, folded the paper and slipped it in my robe pocket.

The afternoon was less structured than the morning. Some people rested in their rooms while others sat and played cards in the common area. After dinner I spent my time paging through out dated issues of magazines I found in a rack at the far end of the ward. The guy I met at lunch sat next to me on the short couch, and we continued our conversation about writing. My nurse, noticing us sitting together, walked down the hallway and motioned for me to join her. She told me not to socialize too much with the other patients. She suggested I take a shower before I went to bed, so I would be ready to meet with a team of doctors in the morning for an interview.

She unlocked a shower area, handed me a single pack of shampoo and told me she would be right outside the door. I peeled off my pajamas, robe and booties. The warm spray flowed over my hair and ran down my body. For the first time in days, I felt relaxed and almost normal. After the shower I pulled on my pajamas and wrapped my robe around me. When I opened the door, my nurse was waiting for me. She put her arm on my shoulder. "How did the shower feel?"

"Great, like a day at the spa." She smiled at me and we walked back to my room. My roommate had checked out earlier in the day, so I had the room to myself. The nurse helped me into bed and asked how my day went. I told her I thought the day went well, and I felt more relaxed than I had in a long time.

"That's good, Diane. In the morning you'll meet with a team of doctors who will ask you a few questions and talk to you about your progress. Just relax and answer their questions as honestly as you can. They will decide if you're ready to move to a regular room and participate in some group counseling sessions that will help you work through your depression." She handed me my medication and patted me on the arm. "You'll do fine." I swallowed the pill and handed the plastic cup back to her.

The next morning, shortly after breakfast, the nurse stopped in my room with my clothes. While I dressed she waited for me in the common area. After almost three days in the hospital my black cotton pants and sweatshirt filled me with energy. The nurse had even brought me my purse, so I could put on some makeup for the interview. When I met my nurse in the common area, she put her arms on my shoulders and said, "You look great. Remember, relax and just answer their questions."

She led me to a small conference room where two expressionless people sat at a long table. A man, dressed in a brown plaid sport coat and tie, sat next to an older woman, dressed in a drab jacket with a beige blouse. They both had manila folders in front of them. They motioned for me to sit in the chair across the table from them. The man folded his hands in front of him and asked me my name and why I was in the hospital. I told him about my husband's death, the trauma of trying to resuscitate him, and that John was all I had. They asked me if I had children. I told them no and that I lived alone.

The woman asked a few more questions and then a silence fell over the room. I tried to sit still in my chair and I kept my hands in my lap while they studied their notes. Finally, the woman said, "Well, Diane, based on the nurse's notes and what you said today, we'll have you moved to a regular room for inpatient counseling. Keep up the good work."

I smiled and thanked them. My nurse was waiting for me outside the door. She looked at the smile on my face and hugged me. We walked back to the common area and sat down on the couch. She told me to stay dressed and that she would let me know as soon as she received my room assignment. Later in the afternoon, the nurse brought me my coat and other belongings and said my room was ready. Before the sliding glass door opened, she hugged me. She said she was sorry about my husband and told me to take care of myself. I hugged her back and thanked her for all her help.

The room was a typical hospital room with two beds and a bathroom. When the nurse and I walked in, my new roommate, with hair pulled back in pigtails and wrapped with red ribbons, closed her magazine and grinned. The nurse hung my coat on a hanger. Outside the window, snowflakes filtered through the air and settled on cars parked on the street below. After the nurse left, my roommate explained how the television worked. Unlike my first room, this one had a telephone between the two beds.

My roommate decided to visit a friend down the hallway and invited me to join her. I told her to go ahead, that I had a few phone calls to make. After she disappeared out the door, I called my sister to tell her I had moved to a new room and would be in the hospital a few more days. She asked if I needed anything. I asked her if she could stop at the house and pick up a change of clothes for me. As always, my sister was there for me. She said she would drive down to visit me in the morning after the kids left for school.

During the days in the hospital, I lost track of time and suddenly realized the get together at my house for my university students was just a few days away. I had to call them and cancel it, but I didn't have their phone numbers with me. Struggling to remember their last names, I visualized the thirty students sitting in class and tried to remember any last name I could. Finally, one student's name clicked. I pulled the phone book out of the drawer and flipped to the "P" entries. My finger raced down the columns and landed on three names that matched. Using the addresses I eliminated two of the three entries. I dialed the phone number and a man's voice answered. It was the motorcycle guy from class. He greeted me with a cheerful hello. When I explained that I was in the hospital and needed to cancel the get together, he offered to e-mail the other students and let them know. I apologized for having to cancel and thanked him for all his help. He told me how much the class sessions had helped him and to take care of myself.

As soon as I hung up the phone, my roommate appeared at the door. She offered to give me a tour of the floor. She walked me past the nurses' station, through the patient lounge and showed me where the showers were. On the way back to our room we each took a chocolate ice cream from the snack cart. Sitting on our beds, my roommate informed me that she would not need to use "our" bathroom much because she wore diapers. When we turned the lights out that night, she said she was afraid of the dark and asked me to leave the light on in the bathroom. I crawled out of bed and flipped on the light.

"Thanks, Diane. You're a nice roommate."

"You're welcome. Goodnight." It had been a long time since I had said "goodnight" to someone before going to sleep.

CHAPTER 18

Tiny Steps

IN THE MORNING we were expected to get dressed, make our beds and show up for breakfast on time. Mary arrived later with a warm hug and a bag of clothes she had bought at a store on her drive to the hospital. I thanked her for the new turtleneck, gray sweater and cotton slacks. She apologized for the basic colors and said she hoped they fit. Assuring her they would be fine, I told her my wallet was locked up somewhere, but I would pay her later. She assured me not to worry about it. After our short visit, Mary hugged me goodbye and left.

I did not see much of my roommate for the rest of the day. The afternoon filled with small group sessions went by quickly. After dinner my roommate announced that she was being moved to another room down the hall. Before the nurse came to pick her up, she wrapped her arms around me and said, "You're the best roommate I ever had."

Then she handed me a plastic sun catcher she had made in the craft shop. "Here, I want you to have this, to remember me. When the sun's out it'll shine through the red bird and sparkle on your wall." I studied the plastic cardinal perched on leaves surrounded by clusters of red berries.

"That's sweet, but I think you should keep it."

"No, I want you to have it, so you'll remember me. Please! Take it."

I held the plastic cardinal in my hand and smiled at her. "Thank you, you were a great roommate, too."

After she left with the nurse, I twirled the sun catcher in my hand and leaned it up against the window, hoping it would capture the sunshine and brighten my days. Wearing the new clothes my sister brought me, I attended the group counseling sessions where we sat around in a circle on folded chairs and shared our stories of loss. The counselors asked questions that triggered tears and forced us to accept the changes in our lives. The sessions focused on identifying stress factors in our lives, strategies for coping with anxiety and living a healthy life. One activity started with the question: You've been staying in the hospital for a short while, when you discover you have been rewarded a "relocation" to a remote island. During the three days before you leave, you may spend time with anyone you choose. Who would you choose and why? I wrote, "My sister, her family and my brother." When it was my turn to share my answer I explained that I picked my family because they had been my strongest supporters since my husband died.

Our sessions also focused on healthy eating. Eating three nutritional meals a day and healthy snacks was a stretch for me considering all the dinners of popcorn, microwave entrees and cartons of ice cream I had consumed over the past eighteen months. When the counselors gathered us for our daily meals, we sat together and said "Grace" before eating. Instead of sitting alone at my dining room table, watching *Friends* on television, I laughed and talked with new friends I had met during the day.

At night, alone in my room, the guitar player's "Amazing Grace" resonated in me as I read the booklets from our sessions. I wrote goals in my reflection journal that focused on using the positive energy in my life. One of the first reflection entries I wrote, "I will pamper and take care of the body God has given me," focused me in a new direction where healthy eating and exercise became a priority. During my nightly meditation sessions, I read passages from the Bible, something I hadn't done in years. That night in the dark hospital room, for the first time since I was a child, I knelt on the hard tile floor and thanked God for his Grace and love.

In the morning before I was discharged, I met with a psychiatrist for a consult. He explained that they had taken me off all the medication I was taking before my hospital stay and asked me a few questions about my progress. Then he wrote out a prescription for Remeron, an antidepressant, that I needed to get filled at the hospital pharmacy. After he explained the side effects we scheduled a few weekly follow-up appointments. Before I left he wished me well and encouraged me to call him if I had any questions.

Shortly after I returned to my room, a nurse appeared in the doorway and said, "We're discharging you after lunch today. I left a plastic bag on the bed for you to use for your personal belongings. You'll get your wallet when you sign the discharge papers." She smiled and left. Standing in the room with the prescription in my hand, part of me looked forward to going home. Another part of me worried about returning to the empty house alone.

After lunch the nurse arrived with the discharge papers and my wallet. "Do you have someone you can call to pick you up?"

"Not really. My brother's at work and my sister's an hour away."

"Do you want me to call a cab?" I hesitated. I wasn't sure if I had enough money for cab fare to Afton, but I had no other option. I told her a cab would be fine. A few minutes later she returned and told me a City Wide Cab would pick me up in fifteen minutes at the front entrance. She asked if I had any questions, wished me well and hurried out of the room. Pulling my red coat off the hanger, I turned to look out the window and noticed the cardinal sun catcher trying to pull sunshine out of the gray sky beyond. I thought of leaving the lonely bird there. Instead, I nestled it into my Pebble Beach sweatshirt in the plastic bag and walked out the door.

I wound past open doors, through which I saw patients stretched out on beds and propped up in wheelchairs. Nurses hustled up and down the hallways. Riding down in the elevator, I watched the numbers light up until the elevator stopped and the door slid open. I stepped out into the busy lobby where people sat on couches reading while others paced the floor. With my plastic bag of clothes in my hand and my purse slung over my shoulder, I stood alone in a corner by the front door. My heart raced as the City Wide Cab swung into the driveway. At 2:00 p.m. on Thursday, February 7, 2002, I slid into the back seat of the cab and set my plastic hospital bag next to me. I was going home.

During the forty-minute ride east on Interstate 94, I studied the two plastic hospital bands on my left wrist. The white one with my name, birth date and doctor's name was faded from many showers; it rested beside the red one with the words "penicillin and sulfa drug allergies" written in red marker. The bracelet I made in the craft shop dangled on my right wrist. As I watched the stores and fast food restaurants fly by the window, I thought about my week in the hospital. The combination of group sessions, medication, a predictable routine and spiritual rejuvenation had helped. Headed home alone, I knew my biggest challenges were still ahead.

When the cabby pulled into my driveway, he commented on the gorgeous view and the beautiful house. The meter displayed $35. I didn't have enough cash in my wallet and asked him to wait a minute while I ran into the house. My footsteps echoed as I ran along the ceramic tile in the kitchen and through the front foyer. I grabbed a couple of twenties out of the safe box in the computer room and hurried out the back door. My breath hung in the air as I handed the cab driver two twenties and told him to keep the change. He handed me a receipt and disappeared down the road. I inhaled the crisp fresh air until the wind bit my ears and drove me into the house.

Relieved to be home, I walked down the hallway to the bedroom. As I pulled my Pebble Beach sweatshirt out of the hospital bag, images of my husband's lifeless body lying on our bed whirled through my mind. Committed to maintaining my healing momentum, I cut my hospital bands off and displayed them on our new bathroom vanity. Then I propped the sun catcher up against our bedroom window, hoping the daily reminders of where I had been would keep me moving forward. Standing in the bedroom, panic and humiliation careened through my body. Memories of the paramedics rolling me down the hallway, the sound of the sheriff searching through the closet and the lyrics of "Amazing Grace" twisted through my mind.

Leaving the disturbing images behind, I retreated to the kitchen and washed down one of my new pills. Then I cleaned out the refrigerator, dumping the withered lettuce, the sour milk and the rest of the chardonnay down the drain. I brewed a pot of coffee and flipped through the mail on the counter that the neighbor had collected during my week in the hospital. On Friday, I called the sheriff's department to pick up my grandmother's gun. When I arrived at the county government center a lady at the information desk directed me to an office down the hall. After filling out a form and showing my driver's license, a kind man handed me the Colt pistol and wished me a great day.

On Monday I returned to work, greeted with "welcome backs" from staff and smiles from students. Over the next several months I attended weekly group counseling sessions at the hospital in Hudson just across the river. Each week before the group started, I met with my counselor individually. We sat in her tiny office and talked about how my week went. Before my major training trips, we discussed anxiety triggers and how to work through them. Exercise, nutrition and rest were always key topics during our sessions. At the end of our last session in May, my counselor complimented me on my progress, told me to keep up the good work and sent me off with a hug.

The psychiatrist at the hospital who was monitoring my medications assigned me to a woman therapist located in Woodbury ten miles from where I lived. We connected immediately. Her kind smile and sense of humor lifted my spirits. At our first session I mentioned my weight gain and fatigue. Considering I was a couple of years shy of sixty and had not seen a man naked in almost two years she figured it was the medication, not pregnancy, causing my symptoms. She wrote out a prescription for a new antidepressant and scheduled weekly appointments for the next few months.

I looked forward to our sessions. During our time together we discussed the bouts of depression that had floated in and out of my life over the years. As a child, people had considered me "overly sen-sitive." Everyday events like watching a Dumbo movie on television or my dad selling our first car brought me to tears. In high school our family doctor attributed my low moods to hormones and growing up issues. I had also experienced a period of depression in the late 1970s after a car accident that left me with permanent damage from a whiplash injury. My therapist and I talked about depression and the unresolved grief surrounding John's death, our struggle with infertil-ity, the loss of my parents and my brother's sudden death. We had frequent conversations about facing life alone and the challenges of entering the dating scene at the age of fifty-six and after twenty-eight years of marriage.

We also spent sessions talking about my job, finances, and how to cope with the daily challenges and stress. She explained how even tragic headlines in the daily paper could trigger anxiety and panic in people, and that many therapists had seen a dramatic in-crease in depression referrals since the 9/11 attacks. Each week I left the doctor's office knowing someone cared, and a sense of calm carried me forward. Following my doctor's suggestions, I focused on improving my health and moving ahead in a positive direction. I purged the refrigerator and cupboards of junk food, replaced my evening cocktails with decaffeinated coffee and started walking ev-ery day.

Shortly after John died, a friend had given me a copy of *Simple Abundance: A Daybook of Comfort and Joy*, by Sarah Ban Breath-nach. Alone for the first time in my life, I set out to find the "Diane" buried inside me. The *Simple Abundance* daily readings helped focus my mind on the positive side of life. I wrote daily "I am grateful for" entries in a notebook, some of which were as simple as, "I am grateful for a day of sunshine . . . an evening of rest . . . a heart that had the experience of love."

At night before I went to bed, I prayed, thanked God for the day and asked for continued guidance. In an effort to connect with other people, I went church shopping. Before John died we had attended

Shepherd of the Valley Lutheran Church just a few miles up the road from us. I had tried to attend services a few weeks after the funeral, but every Sunday I went, I left in tears. With a growing congregation, the church purchased a large piece of property a few miles away and built a beautiful, new church. The first time I walked into the new sanctuary and saw the birch cross hanging in the front, I knew this was where I belonged.

When I started attending the Sunday morning services, I sat in the back at the end of a pew, my escape plan, in case the tears started to flow. For several months song lyrics on the screen continued to trigger tears. Eventually, the upbeat music and the pastor's messages replaced my tears and inspired me to join the church. I signed up for the new member classes and attended the four sessions alone. Then on a Sunday morning, with a red carnation pinned above my healing heart, I stood in the front of the church along with other new members. When Pastor Kramer introduced us, the congregation applauded and welcomed us into the church.

Shortly after joining the congregation, I attended a church picnic. While visiting with one of the members I told him I was a writer. He mentioned that they were looking for someone to write a short column for the church bulletin and asked if I would be interested. I hesitated for a minute and then figured, why not? For the monthly column, I interviewed church members about how Christ had changed their lives. The interviews connected me with new people and helped me reflect on my own faith. I joined a single woman's small group that met every week at the leader's home to study women of the Bible. After our study group, and over delicious desserts and coffee, we shared conversations about living life alone.

During my summer vacation, I even joined a church Habitat for Humanity team. I baked cookies for the crew and donated my time and limited construction expertise to the cause. I helped hang sheetrock, handed tools to electricians as they strung wires and worked on the clean up crew at the end of the day. During our breaks and lunch we sipped coffee together and munched on delicious sweets baked by church volunteers. Sitting on a lawn chair in the afternoon sun, I enjoyed visiting with the other team members, especially the men.

I realized how much I missed having John in my life, and I started thinking about dating. When I read the paper at night, I skimmed the "personals" looking for a match. After clipping a few out, I reread the descriptions, but eventually threw them away without calling. Working in an elementary school where female teachers outnumbered men was not the greatest setting for "date" possibilities. Trying to find places to meet guys I read women's magazines cover to cover. Suggestions like grocery stores, health clubs, churches and professional organizations jumped off the pages. I already belonged to a church, had not belonged to a health club for thirty years and considering I hated grocery shopping, the options did not seem very promising.

With my busy work schedule during the week and traveling to literacy conferences every few months, I spent my evenings cleaning the house, working in the yard or planning teacher training sessions for the week. For a change of pace on Saturdays I would grab my writer's notebook and drive into Hudson to San Pedro's Café for breakfast. After ordering a breakfast pizza I sat at a table alone and drank bottomless cups of coffee as my pen flowed across the pages of my notebook. San Pedro's became my favorite retreat on Saturday mornings and during summer vacation. The waitresses recognized me when I walked in and often asked how my writing was coming.

One Friday night I decided to join a few of my single friends at a local sport's bar for a friend's birthday party. After several drinks they started talking about sex and lack of it. They talked and laughed about "reckless" choices they had made where they ended up with assorted "bugs." Shocked I thought, *Would a man over fifty expect sex on the first date?* The more I heard about the ladies' dating escapades, the less I wanted to jump into the dating scene. Walking through the dark parking lot with the car keys in my hand, my mind kept flipping back to the dating conversation. It had been thirty years since my last date. The thought of starting all over terrified me. Dating was out of the question. I decided life alone was not all that bad.

CHAPTER **19**

The Single Life

COMMITTED TO MY independent life, I forged ahead. I enjoyed making my own decisions and having my own routine. However, as the years rolled along, I realized living the single life had its advantages and disadvantages. As much as I loved my freedom on warm summer days, by the end of my lonely summer vacation I looked forward to going back to work. Returning in the fall, the staff and especially the students motivated me to keep going. For inspiration, I kept a quote from a third grader taped to my computer: "Thank you, Mrs. Hohl for helping me remember my story, I'm going to dedicate my story to you!"

Inviting family and friends over for potluck meals on the deck often filled the lonely days of summer. One night in preparation for a get together with my family and in an effort to eat healthy, I decided to fix shish kebabs for myself and cook them on the gas grill to make sure it worked. After arranging chunks of beef, green pepper and onion on the skewers, I went outside to light the grill. A few minutes later, I noticed smoke filtering out the sides. Thinking some meat residue from the last family picnic was burning off the grates, I lifted the lid. A mother mouse with hairless babies attached to her belly scampered along the edge of the grill. I screamed. She leaped over the edge, dropping one baby inside and another on the concrete below the grill. A few seconds later she returned, snatched the baby off the concrete and disappeared behind the hosta plant at the edge of the deck.

After the grill cooled down I pulled out the grates. Peering into the grill I discovered the hairless baby on the bottom. With a pair of tongs I pinched the crispy corpse by the foot and flipped the dead mouse into the garden. With the leaf blower, I blew all the burnt leaves out of the grill, replaced the briquettes and put the grids back in place. Satisfied with my mouse clean up, I lit the grill and headed for the kitchen to season my shish kebabs. When I opened the grill lid, the flames flicked out. The propane tank was empty. I ended up broiling the kebabs in the oven. To my surprise they tasted pretty good.

Every season presented its unique challenges. One sunny October morning over a cup of coffee, I studied my list of chores: turn off outside water, wash windows, cut back perennials, mulch leaves, clean gutters, take battery out of the riding lawn mower . . ." Considering my beautiful fall days were numbered, I decided to clean out the gutters.

After pulling on an old pair of blue jeans, a turtleneck, a hooded sweatshirt and a nylon jacket, I headed to the garage to gather my gutter cleaning supplies. Lifting the aluminum stepladder off the hook in the garage, I thought about John. We had worked as a team on every home maintenance project, including cleaning the gutters out every fall. With the sun directly overhead, I unfolded the ladder and snuggled it up against the front gutter. The aluminum ladder's spots of dried plaster and dents triggered images of John staining the woodwork in our first house in Minneapolis.

"I miss you, John," I whispered as I grabbed onto the ladder's sharp metal rails. Not fond of heights, I climbed the ladder until I reached the edge of the roof.

"Oh crap, I forgot the hose." The ladder wiggled from side to side as I carefully backed down. I unraveled the hose, turned on the water and twisted the brass nozzle until the frigid stream of water turned to just an occasional drip. I pulled on my rubber gloves and, with the hose nozzle in my hand, climbed back up the ladder. As my tennis shoes stroked each step, the ladder wiggled from left to right. The gentle sway was barely noticeable as I pulled the slippery garden hose along behind me.

I piled the hose on the roof and kept my eyes on the peak as I gently eased myself onto the black shingles. Crawling up the roof, I stopped and straddled the peak long enough to pull the hose farther up the incline so it would reach the gutters on the backside of the house. With the hose secured from slipping backwards, I sat down on the rough shingles and surveyed the roof from west to east. The panoramic view of the autumn valley took my breath away. I almost forgot I was sitting two stories up and had a couple hundred feet of gutters to flush out.

As I grabbed the hose and started to ease my way to the end of the roof, a series of clouds rolled in from the west. I scooted down closer to the edge of the shingles so I could reach the copper gutter. Carefully, I leaned over and pulled out handfuls of the soggy leaves. After the clump of leaves hit the ground, I sprayed the gutter until the black grains from the shingles and the small crumbs of leaves poured out the downspout two stories below.

The wind scattered spray onto the roof and soaked into the seat of my jeans. The gutters seemed endless as the gray clouds covered the afternoon sun and the north wind penetrated my yellow windbreaker. By the time I turned the corner on the angular roof, my butt was wet from the damp shingles, my feet frozen, and my fingers numb from the frigid water trapped in my rubber gloves.

With the last forty feet of gutters left, I lifted the hose over the chimney and dragged it across the short roof that connected the house to the attached garage. With the cold wind whipping through my hair, I yanked the hose. CRASH! I stared at the aluminum ladder on the patio entangled in the garden hose.

"*Now* what am I going to do?" Shivering, I straddled the peak of the garage and surveyed my options. My cell phone was in the house. The mail lady had clicked the mailbox closed over an hour ago, and the neighbors were gone for the day. If I cranked out a scream from the top of the roof, no one would hear me. I sized up the gigantic pine tree at the end of the garage. The trunk appeared sturdy, but the one reachable limb wouldn't support a red squirrel, much less me.

The bitter wind whipped across my cheeks. Suddenly, a scene from an old black-and-white 1950s movie flashed through my mind. A damsel stuck in a burning hotel frantically ripped sheets off the bed and tied them together to make a rope. I quickly unzipped my jacket, removed my sweatshirt and peeled off my long-sleeved shirt. Naked from the waist up, the frigid air nipped my flesh. I pulled my sweatshirt and jacket over my goose bump covered body. Weaving the sleeve of my turtleneck under the iron rod in the gutter attached to the roof, I tied the turtleneck in a loop. Then I tied my sweatshirt to the turtleneck loop.

I rolled over on my stomach and stuck my left foot through the sweatshirt loop and eased my body closer to the gutter, my red hands dragging along the asphalt shingles. I stretched my left foot toward the garage and edged it onto the brick window ledge then dropped onto the deck. Shivering and relieved to be safely off the roof, I wondered if the independent life was really a good fit for me. But unfortunately, it was my only option.

After the gutter disaster, I decided I needed to get out more. I admired my single friends. They traveled alone, played on bocce and football teams, and seemed happy with their independence. One October morning, while flipping through the junk mail at work, an invitation for a fundraiser for a congressional representative caught my attention. A friend of mine was hosting an event for the representative at her house. Interested in education issues, I checked "I will attend" and dropped the response card in the school mail basket.

The day of the event, I drove to my friend's house in Maplewood a few miles from Afton. My friend who was also widowed welcomed me with a hug and guided me into the living room. Surrounded by a room of strangers and feeling a bit uneasy I poured myself a cup of coffee. Checking out the snacks and desserts, I noticed a man standing in the corner dressed in a western shirt, jeans and cowboy boots. I inched my way down the buffet table, hoping to catch the cowboy's attention. His black leather hat rimmed with a band of silver medallions bounced up and down as he visited with people around him. When I reached the end of the table, he smiled at me and tapped the edge of his hat. I smiled back.

A few minutes later, as we sat together on the couch, I discovered he was a retired high school teacher, a Vietnam veteran, a father of three kids and had been married three times. When he told me he lived in Montana, I asked him what brought him to Minnesota. He said his sister had recently lost her husband and he was helping her sort through things. I nodded that I understood what his sister was going through.

When it was time for him to leave, he smiled and asked if I would like to get together for dinner before he headed back to Montana in a few days. He seemed like a nice guy. I agreed to dinner and exchanged phone numbers. He tipped his hat and headed out the door. Watching the feather tucked in his hatband, I wondered if I had made the right decision. The next day he called me at work to make plans for "our date." He asked if I would like to go dancing at the Rodeo, a country western bar ten miles from my house. I told him my dancing was a bit rusty but would give it a whirl. Instead of going out for dinner, he offered to fix shrimp and pasta at my house. Without thinking, I said that would work.

The night of our date, I rushed home from work, changed into tight dancing jeans and waited for the cowboy to arrive. When his car pulled into the driveway, I panicked. Knowing it was too late to back out, I opened the door and greeted him with a smile. Standing over the stove my date boiled pasta and sautéed shrimp while I tossed the salad. I kept staring at his back, wondering *Who is this guy?* I realized how much of a risk I had taken inviting him to my house and tried to focus on just getting through the evening. Sitting at the table with Montana Man, I twirled the buttery pasta around my fork and missed John more than ever.

Relaxing in the living room after dinner, I told him that I had not danced for years and was not even sure I remembered how. He stood up and suggested we practice on the living room carpet. With his arm around my waist, I tried to follow his quick, quick, long, pause directions. After several minutes he assured me it would be easier with music. When I went to sit back on the couch he suggested we sit on the cozy love seat. Not wanting to encourage him, I said the couch was just fine. With the dance starting at 9:00, we bundled up and crawled into his sister's Jeep and headed for the Rodeo.

Cruising along Highway 61 to Cottage Grove, I stared at the stranger behind the wheel and wondered why he was driving and not John. When we arrived at the Rodeo, Montana Man helped me out of the car. Walking into the bar, the smoke swirled around my head and country music resonated across the dance floor. Both of us ordered sodas. When he suggested we join the dancers on the floor, I worried about dancing without a couple of glasses of wine to loosen me up. On the dance floor he wrapped his arm around my waist and pulled me tight against his body. With Montana Man leading me and whispering the steps in my ear, we two-stepped around the dance floor.

When the first set ended, we headed back to our table. Happy I had only stepped on his toes twice, I felt the dancing had been a success. Considering I had to go to work in the morning, we finished the evening with a slow dance. With his arms wrapped around me and my head on his shoulder, all I could think about was John. After he parked the car in my driveway, he opened my door and walked me to the front door. We stood, in that awkward moment, under the stars. I wanted to just say goodbye and rush into the house. Instead he asked if he could kiss me goodnight. I hesitated, then leaned toward him and pushed my lips onto his. He thanked me for the evening and hoped we could go out again before he left town.

Relieved to be home, I locked the front door and stood in the foyer crying. Montana Man was nice, but all I wanted was to have my husband back. The next morning the cowboy called me at work and said his schedule had changed, and we probably would not be able to get together again. We exchanged e-mail addresses and promised we would stay in touch. I wished him a safe trip back to Montana and hung up the phone. Relieved to be single again, Linda and I spent the afternoon making plans for our next training trip to Nashville, Tennessee.

By the time we departed for Nashville, I had our travel routine mastered. Standing in the hotel elevator, I wondered how I had arrived at this point in my life with so many new people and places. As usual, by the third day of daily trainings buried in information, Linda and I were ready to go home. To celebrate surviving the long week, we joined a group of teachers who had rented a limousine. We told the driver we wanted to go to the best place in Nashville for dinner. He suggested a restaurant, famous for their steak and lobster.

We piled into the limo and headed for downtown Nashville, sipping champagne. Seated at a long table, we studied the menu. The waiter filled our water glasses and fluffed our napkins onto our laps. We ordered a round of drinks then toasted our new friendships and the end of another exhausting week. After a delicious steak and shrimp dinner, we sat in the bar and listened to the piano player roll his fingers across the keys as he sang songs of love. His blue eyes reminded me of my husband's.

At the end of the set, I decided to buy his CD. I wiggled my way through the tables and stood by the grand piano, digging in my purse for my wallet. When I told him how much I enjoyed his music a smile spread across his face and a warm flush ran up my cheeks. Wondering where my friends had gone I sprinted out of the restaurant and slipped into the limo clutching the CD in my hand. My friends smiled and joked about me "hitting on the piano player."

When we returned to Minnesota, the chick-a-dees' spring song welcomed us home. Drops of melting snow splashed on the patio as I continued to sift through my life. One night, a Memorial Day car sale commercial on television caught my eye. Figuring it was time to finally let go of John's car, I jotted down the name of the dealership. The next morning, I emptied the Eagle Vision's glove box, cleared out the trunk and wiped the dust off the dashboard.

On Memorial Day, with the car title tucked in my purse, I drove to the dealership. A friendly car salesman greeted me the minute I walked in the door. I told him I was looking for a car similar to my Probe with a hatchback and a sporty look. He thought for a minute and said he had a red Toyota Celica GT-S on the lot with only twelve thousand miles on it. He offered to show it to me. Wandering through the lot he stopped by a shiny red car. "Well, here she is. She's in great condition, lots of extras."

He pointed out the leather seats, hatch back, and the 36 miles per gallon highway mileage. "Would you like to take it for a trial spin?" Within seconds, I slid into the bucket seat and we were off. The car handled great and felt like a perfect fit. I followed him back into the showroom. Within an hour I had traded John's car in and scribbled my signature on the layers of sales agreement papers. Driving the Celica home that day, I felt a piece of myself finally fall into place.

When I arrived home, I called Mary to tell her about my new car. Happy for me, she asked what I planned to do with the Probe. I told her, I would probably sell it. Mary thought the Probe might be a good car for my niece, now that she was headed for college. A few hours later, Al called back and said they wanted to buy the car, but not to say anything to my niece, because they wanted it to be a surprise. Happy the Probe would still be in the family, I promised not to say a word.

On Tuesday morning, when Linda and my principal looked out the window at my shiny new car, their faces lit up. At stoplights, people turned to look at the sporty red vehicle. One morning on my way to work, feeling like a teenager, with the radio cranked up and sunroof open, I exited off of Interstate 94. Heading down Mounds Boulevard, I looked in my rearview mirror and noticed two red lights flashing behind me. Thinking the officer wanted to swing around me, I pulled onto the shoulder and waited for the police car to pass by my window. Thinking he had turned off on a side street, I checked my side mirror. My heart slammed in my chest as the officer strutted toward my window.

"M'ame, do you know how fast you were going?"

I thought for a second. "Around thirty, sir?"

"Well, you were *actually* going forty-three in a thirty." I was shocked. *How could that be?* I tried to explain that I had never had a violation. He was young enough to be my son, so I hoped he would think of me as his mother and let me off with a warning. No luck, he wrote out the ticket, ripped it off his pad and told me to slow down. Trembling, I slowly pulled out into traffic. Feeling like a teenager was one thing—driving like one had cost me a hundred and forty dollars, but worst of all I had ruined my perfect thirty-year driving record.

The memory of the red lights flashing in my rearview mirror forced me to stay within the speed limit. I thought maybe the ticket was God's way of helping me become my own person. Embracing my single life, I focused on finding "Diane." On Saturday mornings I drove to San Pedro's Café across the river in Hudson for breakfast. While sitting alone I wrote, consumed endless cups of coffee and filled my notebook with memories of John.

Being single for the first time in my life required stamina and courage. Late one Saturday night when my best friend was out of town, I decided to go to the movie *Must Love Dogs* at the local theater. With only a few cars in the parking lot I moved quickly through the ticket line. With a bag of buttered popcorn and a diet soda, I snuggled into my seat. In the dark theater, I laughed as the divorced forty-year-old preschool teacher stepped into the dating scene. As the movie went on, her fears and challenges trigged tears inside me. Driving home I thought about the preschool teacher and the emptiness of my life. Maybe life alone was *not* the answer.

CHAPTER **20**

The Piano

WORKING LONG HOURS and with the weekends filled with outside projects, I often found myself dusting in the dark. One night as I gently dusted the pecan finish of John's piano, I decided it was time to sell it. In the morning, I shuffled through a pile of papers in my computer room and dug out the consignment forms I had filled out almost a year ago. After signing the forms, I slipped them in the mailbox. A few days later Schmitt Music called and told me to contact the piano movers to schedule a pick-up time. My stomach flipped. I could not believe I was actually going to let John's piano go.

I picked up the phone and tapped the numbers into the phone pad. A kind voice answered, "Good afternoon, Manny's Piano Movers, this is Paula. What can I do for you?" I froze for a moment, my words stuck in my throat. A panic raced through me as I struggled to spit out my scrambled thoughts.

"I need to schedule a time to have a piano picked up."

"Is it a baby grand or an upright?"

"A Sohmer upright."

"I'll check the guys schedule. Can you hold?" I nodded my head. "M'ame, can you hold?"

"I'm sorry, yes, I can hold."

The irritating rock music thumped against my ear. Hanging on to the receiver, my mind flashed back to 1977. I saw John leaning over the keyboard of a Steinway grand piano in Schmitt's Music showroom. His fingers rolling out a few bars of "New York, New York." The memory seemed so long ago.

The voice finally returned. "Sorry it took so long. The guys can pick it up this Saturday, sometime between noon and four. Will that work for you?" I hesitated. *Was I doing the right thing?* The woman at the end of the phone needed an answer. I finally choked out a "yes." She took my name, address and phone number. I said goodbye and stood in the kitchen, empty and numb.

Alone in the living room, I studied John's beautiful piano. I remembered us sitting side by side on the piano bench with our hips touching as he played his favorite songs, and we sipped wine late into the darkness. He didn't play it often, but I knew by the way his hands stroked the keys that it brought him pleasure. He loved his piano almost as much as he loved me.

I wrestled with the final separation all week. Sleep escaped me. Saturday arrived overcast and gray with the autumn rusts and yellows embroidered throughout the valley. I awoke with a familiar knot in my stomach, the pain of separation. By early afternoon, the day was filled with sunshine and blue skies. My spirits lifted. I knew I had made the right decision. John would want me to move on and build a new life. There was no way I was ever going to take piano lessons and commit to daily practice sessions. The only thing I could plink out on the piano was the melody for "The Farmer in the Dell." Yes, it was time for the piano to find a new home.

Reading my *Best Places to Retire* book, I heard the truck's tires rolling down the concrete driveway. The huge red letters, "MANNY'S Piano Moving," jumped off the back door of the truck. Surprised that they had arrived so soon, I wasn't prepared. I opened the front door and a young, muscular guy with dark hair and two cell phones clipped to his belt stepped into the foyer.

"Well, hello, how are you doing today?"

"Okay, I guess."

"Just okay on this beautiful day?" I stood up and looked at the truck idling in the driveway.

I nodded. "Yeah, it's my husband's piano. He died."

"I'm so sorry." He glanced back as his partner walked in and gently closed the screen door behind him. He was slighter in build, had a double-pierced ear and a blond crew cut.

"Where's the piano?" he asked as he looked around the foyer. I pointed to the living room.

"This is a beautiful piano. Why are you selling it?"

My heart pounded and my voice shook. "I don't play. I thought someone else could enjoy it." I swallowed hard. Tears gathered in the corners of my eyes as the two young men marched out to the truck, rolled a dolly down the ramp and into the living room.

"You're sure you want to get rid of it?" The young, dark-haired guy asked as they threaded the heavy leather straps around the ends of the piano. Without looking up, I nodded. The large straps cradled the pecan body as the two young guys hoisted the piano onto the dolly and began to wheel it out to the truck. I started to cry as John's piano rumbled across the ceramic foyer.

"Take care of it."

"We'll do our best." My muffled cry turned to sobbing as I watched them roll the piano toward the front door. The dark-haired guy stopped. "Are you sure you want to let it go? Maybe a grand-daughter would like it or someone in the family. It's a beautiful piece, excellent shape, won't last long on the showroom floor in the Minnetonka store."

I dragged the back of my hand across my eyes, trying to dry them before I looked up. "I don't have any grandkids. We were never able to have children." They pushed the piano and all the memories out into the autumn sunshine. Before the door slammed closed, the dark-haired guy turned to me again. "You don't have to let it go."

I started to sob. "I didn't want it this way. I didn't want him to die."

I pushed my face into my hands as they wrapped the piano in

a packing blanket and pushed the carefully wrapped bundle up the ramp and into the truck. As the younger man pulled the truck gate shut, the dark-haired guy came back and stooped down in front of me. He reminded me of my nephew.

"M'ame, you *don't* have to get rid of it. We can bring the piano back in. I've had this happen before, but it's never pulled at my heart like this." I sniffled, wiping the tears from my face.

I hesitated and said, "Just take it." He looked down at the tile.

"You can get it back, really, if you change your mind just call Schmitt's. But a beautiful piece like this won't last long. Sure you're going to be all right? Do you have someone you can call?" I looked down at my hands and nodded. He stood up and gently closed the door. I watched the truck pull away. The giant red letters disappeared into the autumn afternoon.

"What have I done?" I screamed as I looked at the huge void along the living room wall. I was not sure which was bigger, the empty space on the wall or the hole in my heart. I cried, screamed and paced the floor. *Why did I let his piano go!* I ran to the kitchen and grabbed the portable phone. My hands shook as I read the numbers off the sticky note on the counter and punched the buttons for Manny's. Eternity passed by as I waited for a voice at the other end to answer.

"Manny's piano movers."

The moment I heard the familiar voice, I sobbed into the phone, "Two of your guys picked up my piano a few minutes ago. It was my husband's. He died. I need it back."

"Hang on. I'll dispatch the driver. Don't hang up." Waiting, I paced back and forth from the kitchen to the living room. The empty space on the living room wall yelled, "What have you done!"

"Miss? The drivers will be back to your place in ten minutes."

Relieved, I stifled my sobs. "Thank you so much. I'm sorry, I just couldn't let the piano go."

"That's okay, Miss, glad to help. You enjoy that piano."

Waiting for the truck to return, I sat in the foyer and told John I just could not let the piano go. A few minutes later, I heard a "beep, beep,

beep" as the truck backed into the driveway. The bright red MANNY'S letters smiled at me and my heart lifted. The doors of the truck swung open, the two young guys walked to the back of the truck and pushed up the back door. They hoisted the piano up onto their dolly and rolled it down the plank.

"Hi there, we have a piano delivery for Diane," the dark-haired guy said with a grin. They rolled it through the foyer and into the living room. "Well, this empty space is perfect for a piano, like it belongs here," the young guy chuckled as he removed the straps. The guys eased it off the dolly and gently pushed it back to the wall.

"I am so sorry that you had to come back. I just couldn't do it."

"I knew taking it was a mistake. Glad you called us back. You know, usually when we pick up and deliver the same piano to the same house in the same day we get a free lunch."

"I can order you a sandwich from the deli in town."

The young guy winked. "I'm just kidding, you don't owe us anything."

As they walked out the door, I yelled, "Wait, here is your check for the pick up."

The dark-haired guy looked me in the eye and said, "You don't owe us anything, this one's on us." The delivery truck door rattled and clanged shut. They secured the lock and climbed into the cab. My body relaxed and my heart softened as I watched the bright red letters slowly pull out of the driveway for the last time. I walked into the living room, sat down on the piano bench and ran my fingers along the pecan finish. I was so glad to have the piano back where it belonged.

᪥᪥᪥

With the autumn leaves buried under drifts of snow, I filled my lonely winter nights with sitcom reruns, *American Idol* and hours on the computer. One night a "free trial offer" for a dating service appeared in my mailbox. After skimming the information I decided to give it a try. On my archaic computer system I entered my answers to the detailed profile information, set up a password and clicked "done." Within seconds a message welcoming me to the world of online dating appeared on my screen.

Dating in the twenty-first century was nothing like bar hopping in the 1970s. Sitting in front of my computer screen in my pajamas, I sipped coffee and studied potential mates' profiles. The image in my head of my "soul mate" was a six-foot-two man, late fifties, educated, a nonsmoker and with hair, even if it was gray. Not wanting to move to Tahiti or Nova Scotia, I limited my search to the United States. Every night I skimmed through profiles with the hopes of meeting that special person. Within a few weeks I connected with several guys, a few from the Twin Cities and two others from California and New York.

Every time one of their messages showed up on my profile my stomach fluttered. Late into the night I read their messages and "chatted" with them. When I told my sister about my new online adventures she seemed skeptical.

"Are you sure it's safe? Are you sure they're telling you the truth?"

"Ah, it's no worse than meeting guys in a bar. At least online I can just delete them."

"Well, be careful and call me before you go out with any of them." I told her I doubted if I would ever actually go out on a date, but assured her I would call if I did.

A few weeks later, one of the guys from Minneapolis contacted me through the site and asked if I would like to meet him for dinner. I knew I had to start somewhere, so that night I accepted his invitation. We decided to meet at The Broiler, a local café just a few blocks from where John and I lived in Saint Paul. The morning of the date, I tried several outfits on before deciding on a pink cashmere sweater and gray wool slacks. I thought about the date all day. After work I called my sister to let her know where I was meeting my date and that I would call her when I got home.

When I arrived at The Broiler, I eased the Celica into a parking space and headed for the front door of the diner. A tall man wearing a gray wool overcoat with his hands stuffed in his pockets stood by the door, staring out the window. When I walked in he smiled at me and shook my hand. After an awkward hello and brief introductions we followed the waitress to a table for two. She handed us paper menus and said she would be back in a minute to take our order.

Visiting over coffee, I found out he had just moved to Minnesota from Colorado and was living in a buddy's basement until he found a job. I didn't remember reading *that* on his profile. Both of us ordered soup and salad, a red flag that this was going to be a short date. After the salty soup and more than enough coffee, we decided to call it a night. I pulled out a ten-dollar bill to pay for my meal, but he insisted on paying. Before walking out into the cold night air he gave me a hug, and I thanked him for the evening.

When I got home I called my sister and told her that the date went okay, but no sparks flew between us. In the morning his "nice evening . . . best wishes" e-mail confirmed my thoughts. A bit disappointed but relieved I grabbed my lunch and headed for work. I thought maybe a different dating site would work better. That night I signed up for another online dating service that claimed it would find the love of my life.

CHAPTER **21**

On the Road

THE 2004 SPRING sunshine finally broke through the overcast Minnesota sky. Sitting on the patio, I soaked up the warm rays as melting snow trickled down the gutters. Committed to leaving the romantically uneventful winter behind me, I planned a summer road trip to Montana to visit my cousin who lived in a small town near Billings, Montana. When I was a child his sister and I had spent weeks at a time at each other's house during summer vacation. They lived in the country in northern Minnesota and my family lived on Long Lake in New Brighton, Minnesota. I enjoyed visiting my "country cousins" and we became very close over the years.

Excited about my Montana trip, I called AAA for travel information and to reserve a hotel room in Bismarck, North Dakota. The morning of my trip I loaded the Celica with enough clothes and gear to get me all the way to the Pacific coast. Cruising along Interstate 94 through North Dakota I pushed the gas pedal down until my speedometer registered ninety miles per hour. My exhilaration came to an abrupt halt when I saw a highway patrol officer at the side of the road, writing out a ticket. My foot automatically backed off the gas pedal. The last thing I needed was another speeding ticket. I set my cruise at seventy-five.

In spite of the weather and stopping at almost every rest stop between western Minnesota and Bismarck, the first seven hours zipped by. Driving through the rain and mist I arrived at the motel the AAA woman had booked for me. I studied the "Inn" from inside the car and reread the "three star" description in the tour book. The young fellow at the front desk, happy to have some business, welcomed me and slid the room key across the counter.

After checking out my $35.99 room that looked like a closet with a cot and a toilet, I returned to the front desk to see if I could get a different room. The guy said they had larger rooms with king sized beds on the backside of the building, but the rooms cost more. When I asked him how much more he studied his list and said, "Four dollars." I told him I'd take it. Wheeling my suitcase into my new room I noticed an odd odor. The room did not seem all that clean, but for one night I figured it would be fine. After a dinner alone at Famous Dave's I returned to my deluxe room for a soothing bath and a can of diet soda. Flipping through the channels I found an episode of *Friends* to watch while I polished my nails.

Exhausted from the drive, I crawled into the king sized bed, anticipating a luscious sleep. But with the air conditioner fan clicking off and on, the not so clean blanket pulled up to my chin and the terrible odor filtering through my nose my body refused to relax. I turned on the light and read for a while, hoping to fall asleep. Still awake at four a.m., I packed up, checked out and pointed the Celica west. Shortly after sunrise a sign for Theodore Roosevelt National Park caught my attention. I pulled the Celica into the parking lot filled with the whir of semi-trucks idling behind me. Before leaving, I walked along the vista hiking paths and clicked a few photos of the badlands.

Back in the car, I set my sights on Billings, Montana. Between Teddy Roosevelt's park and the gas station in Billings I made several rest stops, some more urgent than others. After filling up the car with gas, I called my cousin. He gave me directions to his house. As soon as I pulled into the driveway he welcomed me with a big Montana hug. Over the next several days, we enjoyed visiting over endless cups of coffee in the morning. After dinner, as we sat on the deck under the Big Sky stars, we shared stories of our single life and our hopes for the future.

My cousin, a wonderful host, planned to show me all the sites he could in a week. One morning my cousin, his son and I packed a few basic supplies into his van and set out for Yellowstone National Park. Winding up the Beartooth Highway I understood why it was considered one of the most beautiful drives in the United States. The steep elevation and frequent switchbacks revealed gorgeous vistas of snow-capped mountains and pines in every direction. The van zig-zagged from one switch back to another, climbing higher and higher. With my cousin driving, I inhaled the mountain air as my camera captured images of the weathered rocks and mountain peaks capped with snow.

Never having been to Yellowstone, I snapped photos of buffalo grazing at the side of the road and mud pots gurgling out of the ground. We hiked the trail down to Inspiration Falls and listened to the falls roar as clouds of mist drifted above us. Sitting on a wooden bench in the late afternoon sun, we waited for Old Faithful to spew thousands of gallons of boiling water a hundred and fifty feet into the air. We stopped at the Old Faithful Inn to get rooms for the night, but they were full. So my cousin searched out a camping site and pitched a tent for the night. Considering my idea of camping was a hotel with room service, my cousin and his son took the tent and I slept in the van.

After we returned from our Yellowstone adventure, my cousin offered to take me rafting on the Yellowstone River. While he and his son organized the equipment, I drove to the drugstore in town and purchased a six-dollar pair of water shoes. Dressed in swimsuits and T-shirts we piled our gear into the van and headed for our launching spot. Once afloat in the gray rubber raft we drifted gently down the river, sipping our beverages and soaking in the lazy afternoon sun; a perfect ending to a wonderful week with family.

I decided to drive straight through to Minnesota on my return trip. With my Shania Twain CD blaring and the sunroof cranked open I whipped past familiar landmarks and town signs posted along Interstate 94. As Shania's song, "Forever and For Always," echoed through the car, tears filled my eyes. My trip to Montana had been a wonderful break from the loneliness, but I knew when I arrived home John would not be there.

Focusing on the music, I munched chips and sipped my diet soda. Anxious to get home I lost track of my speed. Shortly after I crossed the North Dakota border into Minnesota, red lights appeared in my rearview mirror. I pulled over, hoping to see the highway patrol car flash by. When the officer appeared at my window, I handed him my license and explained that I had left Billings early that morning and was tired from the long drive. He glanced at the chips on the seat and studied the Yellowstone hat on my head. He handed my license back and let me go with a warning to slow down. Easing back into traffic I wondered if buying this sporty red car had been the right decision. Hoping to stay out of trouble, I set the cruise control on sixty-five and stayed in the right lane while vans and trucks with boat trailers whipped by me. Shania's song, "Up," gave me hope that my life, in spite of the challenges, would eventually get better.

For one last getaway before school started in August, I rented a condo at Bluefin Bay, a resort in Tofte, Minnesota, a small town perched on the edge of Lake Superior. The Ojibwe Indians named the lake "Gichigami," which means "big water." Considered one of the largest fresh water lakes in the world, Lake Superior stretches 350 miles in length and measures 1,300 feet deep. Having taken numerous trips to the North Shore as a child to visit my great aunt who owned a cottage on the lake, and later with John, the North Shore had always provided me with peace and relaxation. After John died, Bluefin Bay Resort became my solitary haven where I could write, hike and enjoy the lake's ever-changing personality.

Shortly after arriving at Bluefin Bay, the spirit of the wilderness captured me. Barely settled into my condo, I hiked to the front desk and signed up for a kayak lesson. Sitting in front of the fire that night, I started second-guessing myself. John and I had owned a Winona canoe for a while, but our limited paddling experiences consisted of a few hours of skimming across calm, secluded Boundary Water lakes. Even the thought of just sitting in a kayak unnerved me. When I woke up in the morning I prayed for rain, so they would cancel the class. Unfortunately, the gray skies did not deter our instructor. After the newlywed couple and I signed a waiver in case we were injured or we died, the instructor gathered us on the rocky shore. While I held a double-ended paddle in my hand, he explained the paddle angles, grips and strokes.

When he asked me how tall I was I answered five six. He handed me a heavy rubber wet suit. Then he explained that Lake Superior's average summer water temperature is forty degrees Fahrenheit. He told us to wet down our suits first with warm water, which hopefully would help keep our bodies warm if we capsized. The thought of capsizing terrified me. In the women's locker room, I stripped down to my bathing suit and stepped into the shower. After wetting down my body with warm water, I pushed my legs into the heavy rubber wet suit. Managing to get the first section of the suit up to my knees, I wiggled my body parts back and forth until I finally pulled the bib up under my chin.

When we returned, the instructor handed us windbreakers, life jackets and a baglike piece of equipment that snapped onto the kayak. Lifting one end of the kayak, he asked me to grab the other end. Feeling like an astronaut in all my layers, I struggled to carry my end of the seventy-pound kayak to the edge of the water. With four kayaks lined up in a row, the instructor directed us to climb into our kayak and sit all the way back so he could adjust our rudder pedals. *Great. I have to use me feet, too?* Then he told us to grab the apron around our waist, pull it forward and fit it around the kayak opening.

"If you capsize you need to pull this loop to detach yourself. Then hang on to the kayak, no matter what. It's your only floatation device, except for your life jacket."

Capsize? Tip over? I worried about finding the ring and getting trapped under the kayak. Our instructor launched his kayak into the clear frigid lake yelling, "Now remember your five strokes. Forward . . ." His voice faded into the vast blue water in front of us. I panicked. *What did he say? Are there FIVE strokes?*

Trembling, I floated out onto a massive lake capable of throwing ten-foot waves during a November storm. Boulders resembling giant turtles appeared below the lake's clear surface. We cruised along the calm water, admiring the rocky shoreline speckled with tattered fish houses. Paddling harder, I floated farther out into the open water and stroked through the gentle late morning swells. Our instructor glided along the smooth surface with ease as he pointed out landmarks and told us stories of the wreck of the *SS Edmund Fitzgerald*.

With the sun sparkling on the lake's serene surface, I tried not to think about the huge waves that crashed over the ship's rail and the twenty-nine men who died. My arms ached from the paddling and my feet continued to confuse left and right, but the lake's beauty pushed me forward. I felt a new sense of strength flow over me. I thought about how much my professional life had grown with the support of my colleagues, especially Jane and Linda. I realized how much my travel experiences—alone or with others—had enriched my life and how much I enjoyed meeting new people along the way. I had even become more confident in tackling home maintenance chores.

Skimming across the water, an image lingered in my mind of the rustic log cabin I rented at Sugar Beach Resort in Tofte, Minnesota, in 2002, on my first trip alone to Lake Superior. I could see the cozy screen porch, the old paddle lock on the heavy front door and hear the ripple of the waves beyond the living room. Alone, I had slept with all the windows open, a gentle breeze and a full moon had kept me company, as the waves tickled the edge of the rocky shore. Paddling my kayak along Lake Superior, empowered by the realization that I *could* make my own decisions and meet challenges with or without a man in my life, I stroked faster and harder gliding smoothly into the pebble-covered shore.

Sitting alone at dinner, I savored the excitement of my kayaking experience. My trip to Montana and the morning paddling around Lake Superior with three strangers assured me that I could live an independent life. Yet watching the gray-haired couple sitting in the corner holding hands made me miss John more than ever. Sitting alone on the condo deck, a peach-hued moon glistened across the water as the "what ifs" and my husband's smile filtered through my mind. I knew John wanted me to be happy and enjoy my life.

In the morning, sitting on a boulder by the lake, the aroma of morning fires filtered through the air while gulls swooped above and begged for scraps of bread from tourists perched on the rocks. Not wanting to leave, I hiked and climbed on the rocks along the shore as long as I could. Hoping to carry the tranquility and peace of the North Shore home with me, I inhaled the white-capped waves rolling over the lake and snapped photos of the giant boulders just below the water's surface. At noon, I said goodbye to Lake Superior, packed up the car and closed the condo door behind me.

The message light on my answering machine welcomed me home. I pushed the "play" button: "Hey, Diane, what's up? Call me." I had not heard from my young friend Paula in a long time. Our conversations in her consignment shop after John died seemed so long ago. After I unpacked and sorted through a week's worth of mail I decided to call her. After telling her about my Montana trip and North Shore adventures, our conversation shifted to dating. After giving her a detailed account of my online dating escapades, I told her I planned to give up on the whole dating idea and stay single for the rest of my life. After a long silence she suggested I try Match.com. She had met her boyfriend on Match.com and she tried to convince me I was too young to give up. Easy for a thirty-year-old to say; at almost fifty-eight I was finally feeling comfortable in my own skin and after my North Shore retreat living the single life made more sense than ever. Before we hung up she suggested I just try the site for a few months. I assured her I'd think about it.

In October, continuing my quest for independence, my best

friend from high school and I went to a Christian women's retreat in Alexandria, Minnesota. My friend had spent several years alone after her divorce. I considered her an expert on the independent life. During the four-hour drive we laughed and talked about the joys and challenges of the single life. All weekend I participated in activities focused on strengthening my faith and nurturing the female spirit. During our quiet meditation times my mind kept floating back to Paula's comment.

My five years alone had renewed my connection with God and opened my eyes to a future filled with new opportunities. Yet there's something about eating pancakes in a bar on a Saturday morning that makes a lonely heart ache. When I arrived home from the women's retreat, I flipped on my computer and signed up for Match. Under my caption "Teacher Ready To Kick Up Her Heels," I answered the profile questions. Even after five years, marking the word *widow* pierced my heart. In the section about myself I wrote that I enjoyed spending time with those I love, sharing candlelight dinners and spending time outdoors. I described my perfect "match" as someone who was physically active, found joy in each day, and liked to travel. I ended the description with "Life was made to have fun, are you ready?" Waiting for "winks" to show up in my Match mailbox, I wondered if *I* was ready.

For the next few days I spent my evenings snapping photos of myself with my new digital camera so I could post them on my profile. I fixed my hair, put on some makeup and picked out a few outfits for my photo shoot. Then I piled a few books on top of John's leather chair and positioned the camera on top. Clicking the auto shoot timer I quickly slid onto the piano bench and smiled into the camera. I flipped through the images on my camera and ended up picking a photo my friend had taken of me early in the summer. Later that night after reading my evening Bible passage, I prayed for God's guidance. I asked Him if there was someone who would be a good fit for me, to please draw that person to me. If not, I asked Him to give me the courage and strength to live alone.

The next night I tried uploading the photo onto my profile. Having recently purchased a new iMac, I figured the upload would be a breeze. I followed the dating site's photo directions, but nothing was happening. Frustrated, I called the help number in California. A young man's voice answered. After I explained the problem he asked if I had dial up or wireless. When I said dial up he assured me that was the problem. All I had to do was follow the directions on the site and wait a LONG time. He warned me not to touch the computer while I was waiting, and he'd call me back when the photo appeared on the site. Twenty minutes later he called and congratulated me on my successful upload.

Every night after work I rushed home to check for "winks." A few appeared in my mailbox, but none of their profiles really excited me. After adding more photos to my profile and two months of only a trickle of "winks" and a disastrous date with a guy who considered sitting on a dock with a six-pack of beer and a fishing pole a luxury vacation, I told my sister I was ready to stay single and live alone for the rest of my life. With only a month left on my subscription I decided that when the subscription ran out, I was done dating.

CHAPTER 22

In a Wink

INSTEAD OF FOCUSING on finding a man, I poured my energy into the one consistent piece of my life, my job. Not having children of my own had been a major loss for me. As a child I spent hours playing "house" and dolls with my girlfriends thinking someday I would have a real baby to snuggle into a buggy for afternoon walks around the block. Yet I always believed teaching was my calling. For the most part I enjoyed the challenges and rewards of my literacy position. The upward movement of our state test scores gave our staff hope that we would soon get off the state list of "under performing schools." Seeing the improvement in our test scores, a coach who worked with other schools on "the list" suggested we partner up with an elementary school on the Red Lake Indian Reservation three hundred miles north of Saint Paul.

On a Friday in January 2006, Linda and I drove north to Bemidji, Minnesota, to follow up on the August literacy training we had done with the staff. The kindergarten through eighth grade elementary school located on a peninsula separating the Upper and Lower Red Lakes was a forty-mile drive from Bemidji. The traditional Ojibwe tribal community had a Head Start program, a health clinic, elder program, fitness center and grocery store. Exhausted from the six-hour drive on snow slick roads we were relieved to pull into the Hampton Inn parking lot. With the wind biting our cheeks, we dragged our luggage into the hotel lobby. Standing at the front desk we soaked in the hotel's warmth and the north wood's flavor.

We wheeled a cart piled high with our suitcases and training materials past the cozy fireplace and massive windows facing Lake Bemidji. Steadying the load we muscled the cart into the elevator. After settling into our rooms, Linda and I met in the lobby to plan our session for the next day. To avoid the subzero temperatures we stayed at the hotel, ate dinner at the Green Mill and retired to our rooms early. Finding nothing worth watching on television, I changed into my swimming suit and headed for the pool. After stroking through the frigid water, I sat on the top cedar shelf of the sauna and soaked up the heat. Before drying off I eased myself into the hot tub. With my legs tingling below the bubbling water I walked through the plastic divider and into the darkness outside. Snuggling my steaming body into a corner of the hot tub, the stars above winked at me as my breath formed clouds in the winter air.

Relaxed, I returned to my room, perked a pot of decaf coffee and started up my laptop. As I designed slides for my power point presentation I realized how much my life had changed. During the forty-eight hours in the locked hospital ward I never imagined my life would involve traveling all over the country, facilitating teacher training sessions and meeting so many new people. Thanks to Jane and Linda even my computer skills had soared. Tapping away on my laptop I thanked God for all the strength and courage he had given me to keep going.

With only a few more slides to insert in my presentation, I took a break to check Match.com. After logging in a message popped up in my mailbox, "Planenuts has sent you a wink." I clicked through the profiles thinking what did "planenuts" mean? Was this guy crazy or something? His profile appeared on the screen, but he didn't have a photo posted. Reading through his information I discovered he was a widower, fifty-nine years old, enjoyed traveling and was looking for a soul mate. He *seemed* normal, but I needed time to think and decided to contact him when I got home, hoping he would have his photo posted by then.

During the two days of training my mind wandered back to the "wink." We both had lost our spouses, enjoyed traveling and lived within twenty miles of each other. Our paths probably had crossed at some point at the local Fleet Farm or County Market grocery store. His comment "looking for a navigator on the road of happiness" intrigued me. On Saturday January 28, with the last session over, Linda and I packed our suitcases, laptops, projector and training materials into Linda's Ford Explorer and pulled out of the snow-covered school parking lot. Winding along the deserted reservation roads the wind blew and drifted snow across our path. While Linda drove I read the feedback sheets out loud, and we made plans for the next training session. Leaving the rural back roads behind, Linda eased the truck down the entrance ramp onto Interstate 94. Wisps of snow blew across the freeway as the Ford Explorer and the rest of the traffic crawled along in the right lane, following the barely visible tire tracks ahead. When we finally pulled into my driveway, I said goodbye to Linda and lugged my materials into the house. With the aroma of coffee brewing in the kitchen I turned on my computer.

His profile appeared on the screen but his photo was still not there. *Was he trying to hide something?* In spite of the missing photo my finger hit the "wink back" button. A few hours later an e-mail from "planenuts" arrived in my mailbox. Trying to muster up the courage to open his message, I wandered into the kitchen and refilled my North Shore coffee cup. Back at the computer my finger tapped the message button. His message started out with "Good Morning, Diane," which was a positive sign. He explained his unsuccessful Match.com photo upload and offered to send me his profile photo directly.

Trying to follow the dating site's guidelines, I worried about sending my e-mail address. I read through the rest of his message. His wife had passed away on December 17, 2004. They had been married thirty-eight years. He wrote, "Our goal was to be married seventy-five years, we made it just halfway." His message continued, "I really enjoy playing Go Fish and Memory with my eight-year-old grand-daughter and five-year-old grandson. Do they ever kick my butt in Memory!" I thought, how could I go wrong with a guy like this? I decided he was worth the risk.

In my e-mail to "planenuts" I told him the trouble I had had up-loading my photo and suggested he try posting his photo again, but give it a lot of time to upload. I thanked him for his e-mail and sug-gested we meet sometime for coffee in Hudson. Later that evening a "Yippee!" message greeted me. He had successfully uploaded his photo. Staring back at me was a tall, handsome guy in a leather jacket leaning against a black classic 1982 Corvette Stingray. In his message he said he had retired from Andersen Windows Corporation in 1997 at the age of fifty-one, and said he was so sorry about the loss of my husband. He included his e-mail address, phone number and signed the message, "Allan."

After rereading his profile one more time, I e-mailed him back. We agreed to meet the next day at San Pedro's Café, my Saturday writ-ing spot, on the main street in Hudson. Located in a bank building built in the 1870s in the historic downtown area, the café offered a menu filled with spicy dishes, fruit salsas and delicious pizzas baked in wood-fired brick ovens. Their island cuisine menu listed main courses like spicy Yucatan Pork Stew and Jerk Rubbed Chicken. Their Vanilla Bean Cheesecake and Chocolate Habanero Cake, a dense chocolate cake with a touch of Habanero Pepper and warm choco-late sauce, were homemade and impossible to resist. Year round the café was packed with people sipping Golden Margaritas made from fresh squeezed limes, Key Lime Martinis, or on a cold winter night a steaming Island Coffee topped with whipped cream.

After clicking off the computer I thought, *What are you doing, Di-ane? Are you crazy?* I called my sister Mary to tell her about my date. When she answered I explained that he was fifty-nine, a widower, lived in River Falls and his name was Allan. She asked where we were meeting and told me to call her before I left. As always she warned me to be careful and to call her when I got home.

On Sunday January 29, 2006, after considering every possible outfit option in my wardrobe, I settled on jeans and a sweater. At fifty-eight my enthusiasm for the dating scene was dwindling. It took so much effort to get dressed, pour myself into the car and drive alone to a restaurant. To meet some strange guy I knew nothing about. Cruising across the Hudson Bridge, I studied the gray skies and frozen Saint Croix River. This was it, I told myself, if this date turned out to be a disaster, no more dating for me.

Waiting for the stoplight on Second Street to turn green, I checked my makeup in the mirror, slipped a breath mint into my mouth and tried to calm the waves of anxiety rolling through my stomach. As the Celica approached San Pedro's I noticed a tall guy in a black-leather jacket and black jeans standing on the sidewalk in front of the restaurant. "Wow!" I thought as I almost drove over the curb. After parking on a side street, I slid out of the car. Not wanting to look overly excited, I calmly strolled across the street to San Pedro's while my heart hammered against my chest.

After short introductions we exchanged smiles and climbed the steps to the restaurant. Allan held the door open, and we wandered into the café. A few other people who braved the gray, drizzly day sat at the counter soaking in the heat from the pizza ovens and a couple snuggled together in a booth toward the back of the café. Sitting on tall chairs at a table for two, we ordered beverages and studied the menu. When our sodas arrived we both removed the plastic straws and set them on the table. Neither one of us was very hungry so we decided on the café's original appetizer, the San Pedro Ceviche. The menu described it as a combination of lime marinated lobster and black tiger shrimp tossed with fresh cilantro, carrot, red onion and habanero pepper.

While we waited for our order our voices filtered back and forth across the table. We seemed to be hitting it off as we shared stories about our families and our childhood. We talked about our loving spouses, the difficulty of loss and the importance of commitment in a marriage. When Allan said, "Let's see what else can I tell you about myself. Oh! I recycle, and clip coupons," I knew he was the man for me.

When our shrimp and lobster appetizer arrived, neither one of us was sure how to attack it. Together we studied the colorful plate filled with salsa, chips and the marinated seafood. We shook out our napkins and tried to gracefully fill the chips with the salsa and seafood. Scooping the chips into the salsa was the easy part. Our challenge was getting them to our mouths without spilling salsa all over the tropical hardwood tabletops or our clothes. After several chips I gave up and resorted to sipping my diet soda. The waitress cleared our plates and asked if she could interest us in a dessert. As tempting as the chocolate cake was, we declined. When the bill arrived I pulled out my wallet to pay my share, but Allan already had a crisp fifty in his hand.

Before we zipped up our jackets, Allan offered to show me the house where he and his wife lived as newlyweds. The house was just a couple miles up the road in North Hudson. Match.com's safety guidelines rumbled through my head and told me to turn down his offer. Yet for some reason our afternoon of conversation and laughter convinced me to say "yes." Walking on the curbside of the sidewalk Allan guided me to his Trailblazer and opened the door for me. In my mind I whispered an apology to Dr. Phil for breaking the guidelines and prayed that Allan's old-fashioned manners were a sign of an honest man.

During Allan's guided tour of the Hudson area we reminisced about black-and-white television, the Mickey Mouse Club and watching the *Lawrence Welk Show* on Saturday nights with our families. He told me about his two grown sons, how proud he was of them, and that he often picked his grandson up from preschool and took him to Dick's Bar for lunch. I shared stories of my experiences as a teacher, vacations John and I had shared, and my dream of retiring young enough to enjoy the carefree days.

When I asked him what his Match.com handle "Planenuts" meant, he explained that he was an airplane enthusiast. The World

War II P-51 Mustang was his favorite plane, and the roar of the engine cruising overhead was the best sound ever. On our Hudson tour we drove past his first house and the house where his youngest son and grandkids lived. When he swung into the Birkmose Park entrance I wondered where he was taking me. At the top of the winding road Allan pulled into a parking spot overlooking the Saint Croix River. I stared out the windshield at the river below. Sitting in the secluded park I hoped he was only planning to share the gorgeous view with me and nothing else. My shoulders relaxed when he shifted the Trailblazer into reverse and backed out of the parking spot.

Before we headed back to San Pedro's he asked if I would like to see his Corvette that was in winter storage a couple miles away. I thought everything was going fine so far; what the heck, why not? But when the Care Free security gate clicked shut behind us, panic rolled over me. *I should have listened to Dr. Phil.* Standing in the storage unit the shiny black Corvette Stingray appeared a few inches at a time as Allan rolled back the soft protective cover. She was gorgeous!

When we arrived back in downtown Hudson, Allan parked the Trailblazer in back of the Celica. We stood next to my car for a few minutes, talking about our afternoon and how much we had enjoyed our time together. Before he turned to walk back to his car, I reached up and wrapped my arms around his neck. *Honest, Dr. Phil, I had not planned to kiss "Planenuts."* The kiss just happened. Driving home, I kept replaying our date in my mind. The image of him standing in front of The San Pedro Café in his black leather jacket stuck with me all the way home. Riding in his Trailblazer had seemed so natural. Like we were meant to be together and the Corvette was the frosting on the cake.

As soon as I arrived home, I called my sister to let her know how my date went. Not wanting to sound too excited I told her that he was a tall, handsome guy, well mannered and we'd had a seafood appetizer. She was glad to hear the date went well, but cautioned me to take my time and not to do anything stupid. I assured her I would use my best judgment. Later that night an e-mail from Allan appeared in my mailbox:

February 29, 2006

Hi Diane, To me everything went great on our date. We have lots in common and I felt at ease all the time we were together. I was trying to make a good first impression. Did it go ok for you? I really LIKED the hugs and kisses. Hope to see you real soon. Allan

I smiled. I thought our date went well too and suggested we plan a date for the following Saturday. When I checked my e-mail in the morning before leaving for work another e-mail from Allan had arrived:

February 30, 2006

Good Morning Diane, The more I think about yesterday the more positive feelings I get. I really don't want to wait until the weekend to see you again. If I'm trying to go too fast say so and I will cool it, but on the other hand I can kick it up a notch or two. Would you like to get together at Mama Maria's tomorrow night? Have a GREAT day. Allan

I didn't want to wait until the weekend to see him either, but I also did not want him to think I was desperate to capture a man. Figuring I had nothing to lose and my Match.com membership would expire in a couple of weeks, I agreed to meet him on Wednesday after work at the Italian restaurant in North Hudson. On Monday when I arrived at school covered in smiles, Linda asked how my weekend had gone. My smiles must have been contagious, because when I told her about my date her face lit up. A warm tingle ran up my cheeks as I tried to convince her the date was no big deal.

Putting on my makeup before our date, I tried to convince the reflection in the mirror that a relationship was the last thing I needed right now. *Just enjoy it and have fun.* When I pulled into the dark parking lot at Mama Maria's his Trailblazer was already there. I tucked the Celica into a parking space a few slots down from his car, locked my car and hurried into the restaurant. Just inside the door Allan stood waiting for me. His face lit up with a smile. Allan romanced "the teacher" with dinner, flowers and a giant apple. We enjoyed a wonderful evening together. This guy earned an "A" in my book.

Three weeks later Allan proposed to me on a Sunday morning at Hoff Jeweler's in Maplewood Mall and presented me with a gorgeous engagement ring with three oval cut diamonds. On Monday when my colleagues saw the sparkle on my finger and the twinkle in my eyes, they showered me with hugs and wishes. Allan and I shared our news at family gatherings and through long distance phone calls. Our families had been with us through the hardest times and wanted the best for us. They were a little surprised at how fast we had moved, but at our age we figured we had no time to waste.

A few days after our engagement I walked into my principal's office, closed the door behind me and sat down at the same table where he had interviewed me six years earlier. I thanked him for all his support during the most difficult years of my life. When I told him about my plan to retire at the end of the year he said retirement was out of the question. He insisted there was too much training yet to do and that I could not retire. Then a smile crinkled across his face and his blue eyes twinkled at me. A week later, sitting at another small table in the Saint Paul Schools Human Resource office, I signed my retirement papers.

Teaching had been my life. The finality of my signature haunted me all the way home. *Was retirement a mistake? What if the marriage doesn't work out or something happens to Allan?* Six years had passed since John died, but I still thought about him every day. I wasn't sure I had the courage and strength to love someone again. The terror of facing the raw pain and grief of losing another person I loved crashed through my body. I knew Allan was no stranger to life's dark side. In 1996 he faced his own mortality when he was diagnosed with bladder cancer. In spite of numerous procedures, surgeries and several rounds of chemotherapy the cancer refused to leave. Running out of time and options the oncologist suggested Allan go through one more round of aggressive chemo. The chances of the treatment working were slim and the side effects of the potent drug almost killed him. At times the chemo made him so sick that he looked forward to death, but he fought and never gave up. His determination and aggressive chemo worked. The day I signed my retirement papers Allan brought me flowers, and promised he would be by my side no matter what happened.

Allan's commitment to life and his positive attitude were contagious. Focusing on the joy and laughter we brought into each other's lives, our wedding plans soared. Allan wanted to elope to Hawaii, which sounded like a great idea. Yet the more we thought about the losses in our lives we realized we needed to celebrate our special day with family and friends. Being retired we had plenty of time to meet with the photographer, musicians, caterer and florist. One afternoon we met with the owner of the Lake Elmo Inn to sample all the items on our wedding reception menu. A few hours later we were sitting at a "long term care" dinner sipping coffee and eating slices of three-layered chocolate cake. When the invitation to the session had arrived in the mail, we thought the information would be interesting. Plus, we could not pass up a complimentary meal at one of our favorite restaurants. Staring at a power point presentation filled with graphs and statistics about nursing home care, we prayed we would never have to face that decision.

During my six years alone my faith continued to be an important part of my life. Allan on the other hand had not been to church in thirty years, but shortly after we started dating we began attending Saturday night services together. At first it seemed strange to have him next to me in the pew as we held hands and sang along with the band. Listening to his deep voice repeating the Lord's Prayer with me,

I pictured us standing in front of the altar beneath the wooden cross saying "I do."

When I called the church to schedule a date for the wedding, the secretary said we needed to meet with the pastor first and to also sign up for marriage classes. *With sixty-six years of marriage between us why would we need classes?* Figuring a refresher course wouldn't hurt we filled out the registration form and marked the dates on our calendars. On the first night of the class we drove to the church and joined ten other couples young enough to be our kids. Pastor Zach, the associate pastor, welcomed us.

Throughout the evening the young couples shared their anxieties about finances, jobs and starting a family. Compared to their challenges, adjusting to retirement and figuring out our travel schedule seemed pretty minor. During break the pastor suggested, with all our marriage experience, maybe we should teach the class. We smiled, complimented him on what a great job he was doing and refilled our coffee cups. At the end of the fourth session we celebrated our successful completion of the class with cake and coffee.

With the class behind us we focused on the final details for the wedding. On September 8, 2007, at 11:30 a.m. the ceremony began. The white gown my sister helped me pick out skimmed along the aisle runner and swayed back and forth as my brother escorted me down the aisle. At high noon, as husband and wife, we sprinted up the aisle holding hands while the talented musicians from our church, Pastor Kramer and Donna and Eric Bennett, sang "I Saw the Light" by Hank Williams. Allan had chosen the song, a perfect fit for a day filled with happiness.

Snuggled in the Corvette and covered with smiles we sped off to the reception at the Lake Elmo Inn Event Center. The rippling of the fountain and aroma of garlic mashed potatoes, seasoned wild rice and beef bourguignonne filtered through the air as we stepped into the foyer of the Event Center. After Pastor Steve's blessing our guests enjoyed their festival salads garnished with strawberries followed by the delicious entrees of beef bourguignonne and chicken calvados.

The tiers of irresistible miniature éclairs, Lake Elmo Inn's signature chocolate dessert "The Sin of The Inn" and slices of our wedding cake disappeared quickly, obviously a big hit.

ひひひ

As the wedding day became a memory, Allan and I settled into our life together. Blending our lives, we both hung on to photos and memories of our spouses; they would always be a part us. For me, adjusting to a new relationship late in life had its challenges. The six years without John had forced me into an acceptance of solitude and self-preservation that were tough for me to release. During the first few months Allan and I were married, I strived to maintain my independence—a protection against the possibility of losing someone I loved again.

With Allan now in my life, I wanted to build a partnership where we shared our happiness and sorrows. The losses in our lives inspired us to commit ourselves to each other and to a life filled with joy. We looked forward to laughing more and traveling together. Our trips to the pristine mountains of Glacier National Park, the romantic islands of Hawaii and the endless beaches of Cancun, provided us time to experience life again and get to know each other better. We spread our "sparkle" everywhere we went. On our trip to Puerto Vallarta, Mexico, Edith and Arthur, a couple we met there, said they felt a lift in their hearts every time they saw us walking to dinner or holding hands, strolling along the beach.

During my years alone, I discovered a strength and perseverance inside me that I knew would always be there—no matter what. Knowing that loss would happen again, I planned to grasp the morning sunrises like they were the first crimson horizon I had ever seen. I realized, life on earth is a process of sunrises and sunsets; in between you live and breathe what life brings you.

Author's Endnote

Twenty-Eight Snow Angels reveals my personal journey and transformation as I struggled through the grief process, trying to redefine myself as an individual. The book took seven years to write and is based on journal entries, photographs, medical records, artifacts and memories.

Looking back, surviving my grief was not easy; a battle that required determination and a commitment to fight for life. I realized, it is not the time that heals, but what we do within that time that creates positive change. Grief is hard. Little steps lead to big steps that, if we're lucky, lead to leaps. When grief pushes us backward, our only option is to keep trying to push ourselves forward. John's death changed everything in my life, as I knew it. Initially, the pills kept the demons away, but the relentless pain and strength of grief put up a tough fight. Trauma and loneliness almost killed me. It's only through a vigilant battle, the support of others and the grace of God that I'm alive.

Each person's experience will be different, and the coping mechanisms you use to squelch the pain can ultimately destroy or save you. Do what you can to survive and enjoy life again, carrying memories of your past love with you forever. I want others who are facing the loss of a loved one to know you can be strong, capable, resilient human beings who have the strength to survive the grueling process of grief and find yourselves—again and again.

About The Author

Diane Dettmann was born in Minneapolis, and attended the University of Minnesota. After graduating in 1969, she began her teaching career with the Saint Paul Public Schools. Diane was an elementary teacher, a literacy staff developer, attained National Board Certification and is an adjunct instructor at the University of Wisconsin–River Falls. She earned her Master's in Curriculum and Instruction from Hamline University and presented her thesis, *The School of Bliss: A School Designed for Student's Happiness,* at the "Research on Women and Education Conference" in Saint Paul, Minnesota. Diane has had articles published in the *Hamline Education Journal: Herstory of Education* and the *Journal of Finnish Studies,* an international education journal published by Finlandia University. She is currently promoting *Miriam Daughter of Finnish Immigrants,* a book she coauthored with her aunt Miriam Dloniak. She has presented the book at author events, historical organizations and at international conferences in Turku, Finland, and Thunder Bay, Canada. Diane lives in Afton, Minnesota, with her loving husband, Allan.

Diane Dettmann's Website: http://www.outskirtspress.com/snowangels

CPSIA information can be obtained at www.ICGtesting.com
Printed in the USA
269290BV00006B/31/P

9 781432 777043